PASSING
THE
BATON

100 Life Principles And Skills
Every Father Needs
To Teach His Children

GRADY HAUSER

Brian   Martin

Faith Church

May 4, 2014

Order this book online at www.trafford.com/07-1115
or email orders@trafford.com

All Scriptural references from the New International Version, Zondervan, 1978,
unless otherwise noted.

Most Trafford titles are also available at major online book retailers.

Note for Librarians: A cataloguing record for this book is available from Library
and Archives Canada at www.collectionscanada.ca/amicus/index-e.html

Printed in Victoria, BC, Canada.

ISBN: 978-1-4251-3065-7

*We at Trafford believe that it is the responsibility of us all, as both individuals
and corporations, to make choices that are environmentally and socially sound.
You, in turn, are supporting this responsible conduct each time you purchase a
Trafford book, or make use of our publishing services. To find out how you are
helping, please visit www.trafford.com/responsiblepublishing.html*

 www.trafford.com

North America & international
toll-free: 1 888 232 4444 (USA & Canada)
phone: 250 383 6864 ♦ fax: 250 383 6804 ♦ email: info@trafford.com

The United Kingdom & Europe
phone: +44 (0)1865 722 113 ♦ local rate: 0845 230 9601
facsimile: +44 (0)1865 722 868 ♦ email: info.uk@trafford.com

10 9 8 7

DEDICATION

To R.W. Hauser, who passed his baton
on boats, islands, ski slopes and
Mrs. David's lawn.

To Gary, Rick, Dave and John –
my accountability partners for
many years.

The Western World stands at a great crossroads in it's history. It is my opinion that our very survival as a people will depend upon the presence or absence of masculine leadership in millions of homes. I believe with everything within me that husbands hold the keys to the preservation of the family.

—Dr. James Dobson

Chapter 1: Why another book of lists?

Shelves of books have been written to fathers addressing the need for personal integrity and character as we attempt to rear our children. And rightly so, for without these, no amount of contrived teaching and instruction will bring a child into stable Christ-like maturity.

Yet, unfortunately, many fathers who do maintain personal integrity and character still miss those wonderful opportunities, those teachable moments, to transfer their own wisdom and experience on to their kids. The result is young men and women, still in their teens, who leave home one day ill equipped to begin facing life on their own. Too often, it is only after the fact that we realize how many opportunities were missed because life is busy, and we didn't notice the years counting down. To make matters worse, as our children get older, it is only natural that they spend less and less time with us as parents.

This diagram has helped me:

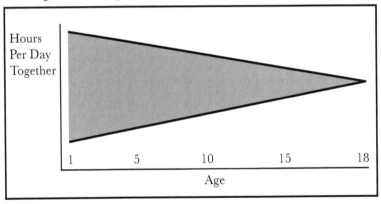

At birth, all their waking hours are spent with mom and dad. A major passage occurs when a child attends school all day. By their early teen years, well, you get the picture. When a young person leaves home at age 18 or 19, ideally we'll have given them all the tools we can to help them start a successful life, and they'll begin working entirely out of their own toolbox.

We can debate the exact angle of the cone and it will surely vary for each child, but it's a sobering thought that somewhere around age 5 or 6, we cross the half way point for all the hours we'll spend together before they leave home.

I'm reminded of Tevye in *Fiddler On The Roof* at his daughter's wedding, when he sings "Sunrise, Sunset...Is this the little girl I carried, Is this the little boy at play...Wasn't it yesterday when they were small?" It sounds so warm and sentimental, but if we let the years sneak up on us, and the window of opportunity to influence our kids slowly closes, we have no one to blame but ourselves. We must always be thinking with the **18-year horizon** in mind. As I plan this summer's schedule, how many summers are left before they are gone?

If I intend to accomplish something specific with a son or daughter, how many years are left? If they are already 13, the remaining 5 years will fly past unless we are always aware of the 18-year horizon.

For some, the years may be few before the kids leave home. Whether you have six or 16 years left with your children, few of the principles in this book will be successfully passed on unless you develop a pattern of time spent alone with them.

How do I get started?

Let me offer some practical ways to create a "connection" with your kids around one of these principles. By the way, plan to discuss or focus on only one principle at a time. It may be a 1-hour or a 5-minute encounter, depending on the particular principle and their interest and age level, but never try to go beyond one at a single encounter. More than one will dilute the value of each. Water spread too thin over a garden will give fewer results than giving just the right amount on a single plant.

1. **Date nights:** Plan a simple event that is a favorite of your son or daughter. If ages are close, you can do more than one child together so long as they all enjoy the same event. Nothing expensive or elaborate required here, just the time and undivided attention from dad will go a long way. Don't wonder what activity to do, just announce a date night for the next Friday and they'll gladly give you their first choice. Then after some time at their chosen activity, stop for ice cream or a Coke, away from home, and share a principle and interact with them about it.

2. **Sleepovers:** When our boys were young, (up through about age 10), a sleepover, where I would spend the night in their room, was a sure hit and an opportunity for great talks by flashlight. It can

be elaborate with a homemade tent, or a simple bowl of popcorn with the lights out. Either way, it is an opportunity for a teachable moment.

3. **Saturday morning breakfast or donuts:** You've worked hard all week and likely haven't had much quality time with your kids for discussing life principles. Again, time alone with dad for donuts or an Egg McMuffin is a great way to set the stage for some of the most priceless times of communication you'll ever have.

4. **Errands:** On Saturdays or any time you have errands to run in the car, take at least one child with you. You'll be surprised how these life principles can come up in the normal course of just doing your Saturday jobs together.

5. **Projects around the house:** Sometimes it is simpler to just do it yourself than to take the "time and patience" approach to involve one of your kids in a project. The time spent together with you, as they learn to model your skills and behavior, can be much more worthwhile than the completed project itself.

6. **Blind date:** A variation on the date night (#1 above) that is a hit with kids up to about age 10 or 11 is a "blind date". Here's how it works. Blind fold the children before you get in the car. Make a few extra turns and stops just to throw them off as you drive to a spot that they will enjoy. This added twist makes even well known destinations fun. And speaking of well known destinations, when you're dealing with elementary age levels, if an event or activity is a favorite, they're not bored by repeating it until about the 50th time.

But even with these connections, often it is not the planned discussion or experience when you hit gold. Rather, it's those unexpected teachable moments that happen when some event triggers the subject, and being familiar with these principles and skills, you're able to capitalize on the moment.

But I'm just not cut out for this kind of stuff

When I was 10 or 11, we thought we could learn to Karate chop boards in our garage back in Boulder, Colorado. Of course, we didn't really know the first thing about Karate, but a 3/8" pine board – we would yell and chop it right in half. Of course, if you were to put two of those boards together, that was a very different thing, and three boards together – out of the question.

You and I are a lot like those Karate boards when it comes to discussing life principles with our kids. The first time we try we may feel weak – like we could be chopped in half. But the second time you'll be a lot stronger and by the third time, you'll gain confidence in yourself and your children will see a new/stronger side of their dad.

If you still don't see yourself as the type to communicate real life lessons to your kids, consider Moses, David, Gideon, Joseph and Peter. Great leaders, but all of them were the youngest, least eloquent, untrained and least confident men around, yet God chose them and used them greatly. You are God's choice to lead and teach your kids.

This, then, is not so much a book to be <u>read</u>, it is a book to be <u>done</u>. It is a practical list of principles and skills for fathers to teach their children, and I hope, some approaches that will help us enjoy the process. If we take seriously the challenge of conveying life's important principles and skills to our children, I believe three things are likely to happen.

1. In the process of reading and evaluating these ideas, we as fathers will begin to see opportunities to influence our children that might otherwise have been overlooked.

2. Our kids will learn many of these concepts at a younger age than most, hopefully avoiding the more painful experience that comes with lessons learned the hard way, later in life.

3. As a bi-product of this effort, your children will see you, their father, in your God given role as leader and mentor. Their concept of the role of a father and their love for you in particular will forever change their own lives, their marriages, and their family relationships.

Table of Contents

Each of the following 100 principles and skills are briefly discussed one by one. They have been divided into four categories: **Spiritual Principles, General Principles, General Skills** and **Financial Principles**. Within those categories, they have been grouped for younger children, early teens and older teens. It's up to you to take the ideas offered here, together with your own, and commit to passing that baton on to your kids. Some will be passed by talking, others by doing, but few will be passed by accident. Deuteronomy 11:19 says: *"Teach them to your children, talking about them when you sit at home, and when you walk along the road, when you lie down and when you get up."*

Spiritual Principles

I.   Elementary Years (ages 5-11)

II.   Early Teens (ages 12-15)

III. Older Teens (ages 16-18+)

General Principles

I. Elementary Years (ages 5-11)

II. Early Teens (ages 12-15)

III.   Older Teens (ages 16-18+)

General Skills and Knowledge

I.   Elementary Years (ages 5-11)

II.   Early Teens (ages 12-15)

III.   Older Teens (ages 16-18+)

Financial Principles and Skills

I.   Elementary Years (ages 5-11)

II.   Older Teens (ages 16-18+)

Spiritual Principles

The fear of the Lord is the
beginning of wisdom.
Proverbs 1:7

The Bible as the Christian's Final Authority

Scripture claims to be God's inspired and definitive teaching for believers. If we accept its plan for our eternal destiny, it is logically inconsistent that we would exercise human judgment to pick and choose from among its teachings for everyday life.

If the issue of Scriptural authority isn't well settled in your own life, don't expect it to naturally fall into place for the younger humans in your house. Without a resolved view of Scripture as our standard, our family constitution, a father's ability to convince a youngster may fade away as time removes your superior stature and control over their purse strings.

The practice of using the Bible as your family authority can be modeled for any age, but when your kids are in 8th grade studying government, use our United States Constitution as an example of what the Bible is in our lives. It is the bedrock document on which we base our laws. The only difference is that God wrote the Bible so it need never be amended. Hebrews 13:8 says that God is "...the same, yesterday, today and forever."

All other spiritual principles we may seek to teach hinge on the authority of Scripture. Unless Scripture is revered, the decisions of what we believe and what we do are negotiable and a matter of opinion.

❑ I choose to teach this   Date Completed   _____

_____

_____

The Concept of "Standing Stones"

You've heard the phrase "That building is a monument to the architect." A building can be a statement, a huge silent tribute to its maker. We build monuments to commemorate great events too. The beach at Normandy holds a monument to the men who lived and died there on D-day. When man first set foot on the moon, we dignified it with a monument there even though no other living creature may ever see it again.

In ancient times, several cultures had the concept of "standing stones." These were inscribed or plain stones, stood upright to create a permanent visual reminder of some significant event. God honored this concept and gave specific instructions to his people on several occasions to erect standing stones, leaving a permanent visual testimony to his actions for future generations. Jacob set up a standing stone at Bethel. Joshua set up standing stones when God stopped the Jordan river and the people officially entered the promised land – some 650 years after God first promised it to Abraham. This concept can even have a major impact on your family and mine.

Let me share my story with you.

Some years ago when our oldest son Colson prayed to receive Christ as his personal savior, we noted the event by planting a small pine seedling in the back yard together. We carefully constructed a chicken wire fence around it so that rabbits, baseballs or other dangers wouldn't hurt it. As Colson grew, so did that little tree, and with it came marvelous and unexpected teachable moments. One day we were watering the tree and he began to talk about someday when he would be grown up and a dad like me. He looked down at that little tree and then over to a mature Ash tree that must stand over 80 feet, and then to me.

I don't know which of us felt more impact at that moment – his visualization of the future or my sense of responsibility as the role model in his eyes.

Even the wire fence turned out to be a spiritual learning opportunity. We protect a young child now for obvious reasons, but when he grows in Christ, someday there'll be no need for a fence and he can be a strong tree on his own.

To give you an idea of how this event took root in the lives of our children, let me continue the story. When we moved from Barrington, Illinois in 1998, our youngest son, Graham, had his own tree which was still very small. But our oldest son's tree had already been in the ground for over 4 years. We all discussed whether to leave the trees. After all, we were only moving about 20 miles away and could always come back and see how tall they had grown. Transplanting them would be a big job and would require a legal revision to the house sale contract since the contract terms were already finalized. I left it up to each of the children to make their decision. We moved the trees.

Plant a tree for each of your kids' salvation experiences. Let the whole family in on the event, videotape it and be sure to do the work together— no nursery deliveries by professionals. Over the months and years, involve them in watering and care of their tree. It will be a 70-year opportunity to teach spiritual truths.

❏ I choose to teach this   Date Completed   _____
                                                           _____
                                                           _____

Using "Grace Cards" to Teach the Concept of Grace

What is grace? I've heard it called <u>G</u>od's <u>R</u>iches <u>A</u>t <u>C</u>hrist's <u>E</u>xpense, or more simply, getting what we don't deserve.

Our sin is a serious matter. So serious that Christ had to die as the once-and-for-all penalty for our actions. This free gift is so great and we are so undeserving that it is hard to comprehend it, especially for young children.

To help teach this most important concept, give your kids an expired credit card. Explain that this "grace card" can be redeemed once, at their choosing, to avoid punishment when they otherwise have it coming. The only condition is they must be truly sorry for what they've done. Then be sure you complete your part of the bargain and truly let them off the hook when they redeem it. Demonstrate the complete forgiveness God gives us when we claim forgiveness through Christ.

From your children's perspective, this simple illustration will come at a time when they are keenly aware of "sin" before you and its likely penalty. That awareness will help them to appreciate the much greater penalty they have avoided because Christ took our punishment and God gives us grace.

❑ I choose to teach this   Date Completed   _____

_____

_____

The Biblical Fool – The Modern Rebel

The Scripture says in Proverbs 17:25 "A foolish son brings grief to his father and bitterness to the one who bore him." Grief and bitterness result from the pain of watching your loved children if they waste and ruin their lives. But additionally, the fallout from their actions may directly involve you, not only in their minor years, but well after they have first left home.

The fool is not weak intellectually. Rather a modern fool would be called a rebel. Someone who resists all instruction, taking long-term actions with a short-term view of life.

Let's draw some contrasts between the wise, God fearing man or woman and the rebellious fool.

God-Fearing	Rebel
1. Believes that the fear (respect) of the Lord is the beginning of wisdom. Prov. 1:7	1. Hates knowledge and instruction. Prov. 1:7
2. Believes and acts according to God's laws. Prov. 10:23	2. Morally rebellious and self-indulgent. Prov. 10:23
3. Saves for the future. Prov 21:20	3. Spends all he has. Prov. 21:20
4. Patient and trustworthy. Prov. 19:11	4. Impatient and unreliable. Prov. 14:16, 26:6
5. Fears God, trusts the Scriptures. Ps. 1:1-3	5. Fears man, trusts PEOPLE magazine. Ps. 14:1
6. Grounded, rooted in principle. Ps. 1:1-3	6. Fickle, life views change with the world's opinions. Ps. 1:4-6
7. Leader. Prov. 17:2	7. Easily led by peers or world opinion. Prov. 14:15
8. Plans for the future. Prov. 22:3	8. Reacts to circumstances. Prov 22:3
9. Heeds reproof. Prov. 9:8,9 Prov. 13:1	9. Rejects, rages, scoffs at reproof. Prov. 5:12-14
10. Listens before speaking, disciplined. Prov. 17:28, 29:11	10. Loves to hear himself talk. Prov. 10:8, 29:11

The list could go on, but this is sufficient to guide more than one discussion when a particularly wise or foolish man presents you and your kids with an opportunity for a teachable moment. At that opportunity, see if they can name any other modern rebels and then discuss what the Bible means in Prov. 1:32 when it describes the destiny of the rebel.

❑ I choose to teach this   Date Completed   _____

_____

_____

God, Man, Animals and Nature. Our Position and Role Among God's Creation.

God has given us a clear hierarchy in Scripture for how we are to relate to God, man, animals and nature.

Genesis 1:26
Then God said, "Let us make man in our image, in our likeness, and let them rule over the fish of the sea, and the birds of the air, over the livestock, over all the earth and over all the creatures that move along the ground."

Genesis 1:28
"So God blessed the (man and woman) and said, "Be fruitful and increase in number, fill the earth and subdue it. Rule over the fish of the sea and the birds of the air and over every living creature that moves along the ground."

Genesis 2:15
"The Lord God took the man and put him in the Garden of Eden to work it and take care of it."

Psalm 8:5-8
"You made him a little lower than the heavenly beings and crowned him with glory and honor. You made him ruler over the works of your hands; you put everything under his feet: all flocks and herds, and the beasts of the field, the birds of the air, and the fish of the sea, all that swim the paths of the seas."

Romans 1:25
They exchanged the truth of God for a lie, and worshipped and served created things rather than the Creator."

Our position and role among God's creation is this: We are to **love and worship** God, **respect** man, and be a **steward** of God's creation—responsibly using and managing animals and nature for beauty, food and our material needs. The primary distinction between man and animals is that we are made in God's image. It is not merely a quantitative issue of our superior intellect. It is the qualitative difference that God built into us, giving us the capacity for moral choices, love, and responsibility.

A prevalent lie often heard in this discussion is that animals have rights. They don't. God gave man both the right and the responsibility to humanely manage and use the animal kingdom for our benefit. Believing that animals have rights is the point, beyond which, all kinds of illogical positions can result. Whether they would put it this clearly or not, those who deny God's hierarchy in nature begin to worship nature, animals and even man as equal players on earth.

It is not necessary to go into all the theological foundations unless your kids are really motivated on this subject. In their elementary years (or whatever their current ages) be sure they understand this word picture:

God	to be loved and worshipped
Man	uniquely created in God's image, stewards of his creation
Animals	to be responsibly managed and enjoyed
Nature	for food, beauty and our material needs

Here is a copy of the scratch pad that resulted when I had this discussion with Colson and Graham at ages 9 and 6. Yours will also become a keepsake, I'm sure.

☐ I choose to teach this   Date Completed   _____

_____

_____

The History/Roots of all Believers from Adam to Your Family

Take a walk through history to illustrate how your family is spiritually descended from great men of faith.

Start with Adam, Noah, Abraham, Paul, Aquinas, and Luther and continue uninterrupted through Wesley, Moody, Graham and finish with yourself and your family. Our kids will benefit when they realize that ours is a 5,000-year heritage that worships the same God who is the same yesterday, today and forever.

God sees no dividing line between his saints in the Old Testament, New Testament, and modern times. To identify with great men of faith as our patriarchs and our ancestors is to raise the personal pride and expectations of our kids and ourselves.

Regardless of your kids' ages, this learning exercise can be fun. We spent one night on each of about 20 major characters of faith. We began with Noah and ended with our family. It took a month or so, but in 10-15 minutes each night before bed, we began to see the seamless picture of God working through average people just like us. Then one Saturday we took an hour and drew a timeline from 4000 B.C. to the present where the boys illustrated all 20 great men of faith, up to and including our family. Try it. The resulting artwork of a six-year-old's perception of fire falling from heaven on Elijah is worth the effort.

Note: For younger kids, the Holy Heroes book pack (p.62) ties in very nicely with this project.

❏ I choose to teach this   Date Completed   _____

_____

_____

Teach Your Kids How to Pray

This may sound so basic as to be assumed, but how many of us have taken the opportunity to talk with our kids about what prayer really is and to give them some handles they can understand and remember? Their observation of you and other men in <u>public settings</u> should not be the only schoolroom for learning about prayer.

Suggestion: For younger children make the bedtime routine one where dad takes the lead, whenever you're at home. Try three models:

1. **Thanking, Praising, Asking**. Everyone takes just one of these three themes and when you've all prayed, you will have come closer to balanced Christ-like prayer.

2. **Conversational.** Guide the children to praying two, three, maybe five times each for just one thought at a time. After a few minutes, thoughtful participation will have come in small, easily learned bites.

3. **Praying the Scripture**: Read a verse or two, then pray a response to that verse. For example:
   Ps 8:1 "Oh Lord, our Lord, how majestic is your name in all the earth." Prayer: "Lord, you are my Lord. Thank you that your name is known, feared, and worshipped throughout the whole earth."

Remember, for us fathers, it is the height of vanity to presume we can lead without prayer in our own lives. We must have the reality behind the image of our leadership in prayer, if it or any other aspect, is to be effective.

❑ I choose to teach this   Date Completed   _____

_____

_____

A Broad Base of Memorized Scripture

When I was single and living in Wheaton, Illinois, I shared an apartment for a couple years with Keith Holmberg. We would leave early and train into Chicago everyday, often getting home late. But partly because of the time that that train commute gave us, we agreed to accept a mutual challenge to memorize two verses per week from the Navigator Topical Memory System. This particular scripture memory tool has five general subject areas, each broken into six specific subjects or truths. Each of those truths has two memory verses that speak to the subject. It's a proven method to help a person memorize scripture – not just by rote, but also by associating two verses with a specific theme. For example, the two verses associated with prayer are John 15:7 and Philippians 4:6,7. It's easy to memorize two verses in this way. Then, with a little steady discipline over time, all 6 themes (12 verses) are memorized as a unit. You can review the verses without ever referring to your printed cards or your Bible, because they follow a logical pattern. In time, all 5 general subject areas (12 verses each, 60 verses) can be learned. The key to this or any successful Scripture memory program is to review it verbally, at a set time, every week..

As the winter months of 1980 went on, Keith and I were motivated to stay on our two verses per week schedule by the high-stakes penalty of having to buy pie if your verses weren't ready Friday at breakfast. Half a lifetime later, I still review a subject (12 verses) at a time when I'm alone in the car. The confidence to use the Word of God in your own conversation or witnessing, and the recalling of key Scriptures in your most private moments, will only result from Scripture deeply imbedded in ours and our kids' memory through systematic review.

The Word of God is…"alive and powerful and sharper than any two edged sword…and is profitable for doctrine, reproof, correction and instruction in righteousness." You provide the framework and whatever incentives will draw your kids into it. In our house, we did this when the boys were 7 and 10 years old. The next page is a copy of the master list that hung on the refrigerator door for months. The incentives were chosen with everyone's participation and significant enough that their motivation never wavered. Twenty years from now they'll still be sharing their faith, and having God's bright light shining into the private corners of their lives because you had a specific Scripture memory plan and you created the motivation.

THE SCRIPTURE MEMORY REWARDS

1.	2.	3.
CHRIST THE CENTER 1. 2 Cor. 5:17　　2. I. 2:20	**ALL HAVE SINNED** 1. Rom. 3:23　　2. Is. 53:6	**GOD'S SPIRIT** 1. I Cor. 3:16　　2. I Cor. 2:12
OBEDIENCE TO CHRIST 3. Rom. 12:1　　4. Jn. 14:21	**SIN'S PENALTY** 3. Rom. 6:23　　4. Heb. 9:27	**GOD'S STRENGTH** 3. Is. 41:10　　4. Phil. 4:13
THE BIBLE 5. 2 Tim. 3:16　　6. Josh. 1:8	**CHRIST PAID THE PENALTY** 5. Rom. 5:8　　6. I Pet. 3:18	**GOD'S FAITHFULNESS** 5. Lam. 3:22-23　　6. Num. 23:19
PRAYER 7. Jn. 15:7　　8. Phil. 4:6-7	**SALVATION NOT BY WORKS** 7. Eph. 2:8-9　　8. Titus 3:5	**GOD'S PEACE** 7. Is. 26:3　　8. I Pet. 5:7
FUN WITH FRIENDS 9. Matt. 18:20　　10. Heb.10:24-25	**MUST RECEIVE CHRIST** 9. Jn. 1:12　　10. Jn. 3:16	**GOD PROVIDES FOR US** 9. Rom. 8:32　　10. Phil. 4:19
WITNESSING 11. Matt. 4:19　　12. Rom. 1:16	**KNOW YOU ARE SAVED** 11. I Jn. 5:13　　12. Jn. 5:24	**GOD'S HELP AGAINST TEMPTATION** 11. Heb. 2:18　　12. Psa. 119:9-11
REWARD: *LAZER ZONE*	**REWARD: *PRO BASEBALL GAME***	**REWARD: *PRO FOOTBALL GAME***

4.

PUT CHRIST FIRST
1. Matt. 6:33   2. Luke 9:23

BE SEPARATE FROM THE WORLD
3. I Jn. 2:15-17   4. Rom. 12:2

BE SOLID
5. I Cor. 15:58   6. Heb. 12:3

SERVE OTHERS
7. Mark 10:45   8. 2 Cor. 4:5

GIVE GENEROUSLY
9. Prov. 3:9-10   9. 2 Cor. 9:6-7

THE WORLD NEEDS JESUS
11. Acts 1:8   12. Matt. 28:18-20

REWARD: CONCERT

5.

LOVE
1. Jn. 13:34-35   2. I Jn. 3:18

HUMILITY
3. Phil. 2:3-4   4. I Pet. 5:5-6

PURITY
5. Eph. 5:3   6. I Pet. 2:11

HONESTY
7. Lev. 19:11   8. Acts. 24:16

FAITH
9. Heb. 11:6   10. Rom 4:20-21

GOOD WORKS
11. Gal. 6:9-10   12. Matt. 5:16

FINAL REWARD: FLORIDA

Keeping Promises Once Made, Even When it Hurts

The Scriptures say in Numbers 23:19 "God is not a man that he should lie, nor a son of man that he should change his mind. Does he speak and not act? Does he promise and not fulfill?" If it is our objective to be more Christ-like and God honoring, then this attribute of God's character is one that should also characterize our lives.

I think there are two sides to this coin. First, there is the obvious strength of character to make good, to be reliable, to be a man whom others can observe and say, "If that's what it means to be a Christ-ian, then I admire that."

The flip side, however, is an equal part as we try to dissect this part of God's character. That is, we should consider carefully the promises we make since once made, we fully intend to follow through. It is a mark of additional credibility and personal character to take time and make the effort to investigate all the circumstances before making a promise.

Whether it is a business contract, an employee hire, furniture at your wife's request or a date-night with your kids, once a clear promise is made, keep it. Breaking it will cause harm in direct proportion to how important that promise is to the receiver.

❏ I choose to teach this   Date Completed   _____

_____

_____

Our House, and Theirs, Can Reflect the Owner's Values

In Deuteronomy 11:20, God's people are instructed to ...teach their children God's laws while sitting at home, while traveling, when going to bed, when we start the day and specifically to write them on the doorposts of our homes. Orthodox Jews have observed the last part of this admonition for 3,000 years. Take this to heart. Spend $8.00 on a 1"x 3" gold plated plaque and have it engraved with "Deut. 11:20". Make it a small family project to affix it above your front door and then teach the principle. The gold does not tarnish, and you'll be surprised, it may create wonderful opportunities to share your faith, and this principle, with guests young and old who pass through your door.

❏ I choose to teach this   Date Completed   _____

_____

_____

The Black Dog – White Dog Principle

You own two dogs. So do I. We may not have any pets in our house, but in a very real way we have two persistent animals that vie for our attention every day. The black dog is our lust for sexual gratification and attraction to pornography. The white dog is our Christ-like desire to be a man of God – to be a man of integrity in our public and private lives.

Every time you feed the black dog, he gains amazing strength and becomes increasingly vicious and difficult to control. To satisfy him, he demands more food, more often, and ultimately like any wild animal, he'll turn on you to inflict pain and suffering on you and your family. The only way to control the black dog is to starve him while at the same time feeding the white dog.

This principle is borne out in Scripture and most other serious literature dealing with the subject of integrity. It's amazing how much weaker the black dog becomes when he hasn't been fed for months. Conversely, the white dog becomes stronger and stronger when we make daily choices to feed and nourish him alone. The Apostle Paul speaks of this principle as our "old and new" natures—our human sinful nature and our Christ-like desire to please Him.

My guess is, if you're honest about this subject, it is an ongoing battle for you right now. How valuable would it have been if your father took the time to openly discuss this with you when you were 11 or 12—when the black dog in your life was not yet at full strength. Here is a suggestion for breaking into this very important subject.* Visit a zoo and call ahead so you can be sure you're at the big cat cages at feeding time. Another alternative is to rent the movie Jurassic Park and watch it together. Either way, as is your usual course by now, do the event without any discussion of the principle. Then, a couple hours later over a Coke, away from home, recall the lions at the zoo or the Raptors feeding frenzy and only then paint a vivid picture of the black dog/white dog principle.

---

* This principle assumes you and your son have already had your discussion about basic sexuality and some of the modern perversions that will fall into his path. See p. 157.

This principle primarily applies to boys and men.

❏ I choose to teach this   Date Completed   _____

_____

_____

The Fear of the Lord

A.W. Tozer, the great pastor, author, and theologian of the 20th century once said, "What someone believes about God is the most important thing about them." The young pupils in our homes will not automatically gain a correct perception of God without our teaching and modeling it for them. That's right, modeling. A child's perception of God will primarily come, for better or worse, as a direct result of their relationship with their human father.

Do we hastily and frequently punish or do we never follow through to discipline when an established boundary is crossed? Both extremes paint a blurred image for their perception of God's character.

The Bible says the Lord is "patient and knows our frame (weakness)", but Scripture is also full of examples where the Lord dealt sternly, especially with those who bore the responsibility of leading others. Look at David. He lost the son born to him and Bathsheba as punishment from God. Moses was not allowed to enter Canaan because of his sin in front of the people. Uzzah was struck dead for assumptively touching the Ark of the Covenant.

The fear of the Lord is the healthy assurance that God will not allow his children to stray into sin very far without pulling us back to the straight and narrow. He loves us too much. Would we let our own children continue to repeat dangerous, childish antics? The neighbor kids are different. We don't have a vested interest in their welfare. So it is with God and his redeemed children. He has a vested interest in us. Unlike the unsaved world, if we persist in sinful activity, sooner than later God's love can be relied upon to pull us back. The fear of the Lord, then, is the healthy respect for a God who loves us enough to follow through in molding us into the image and character of Christ.

So how do we as fathers make this real in the minds of our kids? This is one principle you can't just pull out on a Saturday morning breakfast or even at the end of a date night. Instead, be patient. Wait for the time when your 12, 13, maybe 14 year old disobeys a well established boundary. Then with loving certainty, enforce the penalty, explaining that as their father, your job is to pull them back from the actions that will bring painful consequences in the short or long term. Use that very teachable moment to explain that just as surely, God's love for us will cause Him to pull us back to Himself when we run our own way. His love is even more reliable and consistent than any human father. As a result of this, your kids will grow in their love for you and in a healthy fear of the Lord.

❏ I choose to teach this   Date Completed   _____

_____

_____

New Testament Corollaries to Old Testament Stories

Even with the unparalleled drama found in the Biblical stories, simply reading them with your kids may not be the most effective way to transmit their value.

Suggestion 1: For younger children, start the bedtime routine earlier and create a small drama where you and the kids act out stories that may be all too familiar to them. Have someone walk on the water and save the faithless Peter. Let the prophets of Baal go wild before Elijah prays simply and quietly to the real God. Then let everyone "bring fire down". Build Nehemiah's wall (then let the youngest knock it down just for fun.).

Suggestion 2: Finding spiritual truths in the Old Testament stories can sometimes be difficult, but one approach that often works is to look for the New Testament story or doctrine that is the mirror image of the Old Testament story. God often used Old Testament events to foreshadow the real event or truth fulfilled in the New Testament. These Old Testament stories become even more interesting when we realize they are tied to the spiritual reality that affects us in the New Testament.

Examples:

*	Abraham and Isaac on Mt. Moriah. Genesis 22.	Jesus, God's Son, on the cross.
*	Faith in the serpent lifted up in the wilderness healing the Israelites. Numbers 21.	Faith in Jesus, as He was lifted up on the cross.
*	The Passover—a lamb dying in place of the family. Exodus 12.	Jesus Christ, the Lamb of God, who died in our place (on Passover weekend!)

*	The story of Joseph Genesis 37-47 Future position foretold to him. Betrayed by his own loved ones. Falsely accused. Unjustly punished. Offered forgiveness instead of justice to his brothers. Savior of the known world (18th c. B.C.)	Jesus, beloved Son of his Father.

It is important for even our youngest children to realize that the Bible—all of it—is intended to teach the same truth to us. The New Testament does not supersede the Old Testament with new principles. In fact, Old and New Testaments often fit like the heads and tails, the hand and glove of the same principles and truths.

❑ I choose to teach this   Date Completed   _____

_____

_____

Love in Action

"Husbands, love your wives." These well known words from the Apostle Paul's letter to the Colossians are both an encouragement and a challenge to every husband I know. But just about the time we think we're making progress, a new and different challenge to our marriage relationship appears. It's often the old, familiar issues disguised as some new event. Making forward progress in the "love your wives" category is a never-ending process. The old adage is true in this area: "To stand still is to fall backwards."

But this is a book on transferring life's truths to our kids, not rehashing the "love your wife" issue, you say. I'm glad you asked, because I believe a MARRIAGE CENTERED HOME is the key to our transferring a host of other important concepts to our kids. It's been said that the best way to positively influence your kids is to love their mother.

So how does "loving their mother" play out in the everyday world of yours and my home? There are the tactical evidences like spending time talking and listening to your wife first, before the demands of the children receive your focus. Their observation of this priority will do more good than your direct attention to them. The same idea with a slightly different spin is having a regular "date night" with your wife. The kids should know that as important as they are to you, your commitment to your wife is even higher.

But from a big picture perspective, let me offer three ideas that will give legs to loving our wives.

1. Commit to giving, supporting and facilitating your wife regardless of the response. (As a bi–product, if you truly do it without strings attached, she will eventually believe your actions and respond in kind.)

2. Accept her as she is. You're not perfect either, but isn't it motivating when someone freely accepts you as you are?

3. Fulfill your God given role as the family leader. Do your part to be the man God wants you to be and leave any changing your wife may need up to the Holy Spirit.

If we even begin to make real progress in this area, it will provide our children with security for the present and a role model for the future of what it means to put love in action.

❑ I choose to teach this   Date Completed   _____
                                                   _____
                                                   _____

Worship and Fasting

This is another one of those subjects where books upon books have been written; so let me say again that the purpose here is to offer a few key points to help begin a discussion with early teens. These subjects are often assumed but rarely discussed in most churches and homes, even though they would say they practice both.

Worship: "He worships the ground she walks on." Does that mean he sings a few songs about her and listens to someone talk about the history of this woman? No, our worship is to be our mind <u>and</u> heart – our intellect <u>and</u> our emotions focusing on the persons of God and Christ. A worship service can be a congregation of one or one thousand so long as it leads the worshippers to focus upward. If the focus is on the preacher or singer, we aren't worshipping God. When the Bible tells us to worship in "spirit and in truth" it is telling us to employ our emotions and intellect into dignified worship worthy of the object of our worship. Does **your** Sunday experience meet these criteria?

Fasting: Scripture says that we are to fast in private with no show to draw the attention of men. This privacy element may be part of the reason why fasting is rarely taught, but I think the much larger factor is that we as adults rarely practice it.

So why fast? The history of God's people and specific teaching from Scripture tell us how to fast as part of our intercession with God. There is no question that it is supposed to be part of a growing Christian's relationship to Christ. Scripture teaches that fasting:

1. Can be called for by a spiritual leader of a nation, a church or a family.

2. Can be an individual choice while earnestly seeking God's will or action.

3. Withholds food for some period of time long enough that we are keenly aware that we are feeding our spirit and not our body.

4. Must not be motivated for the praise of men.

5. Must be accompanied by a pure heart and motives for it to be acceptable to God.

6. Is part of a successful strategy to overcome evil and temptation.

Are you facing a particular challenge in your family? Are your children old enough to appreciate the gravity of it? If you aren't today, at some point you will. Look into the Scripture together and then you, as the father, call a day of fasting where instead of eating, you pray together and separately, for God to act in your situation.

Use these verses to establish the importance of fasting as a family and explain why you, as the family leader, may do it alone from time to time.

Jonah 3:5,10 ————— God's response to fasting
Matthew 6:16-18 ————— Our heart attitude about fasting
Acts 13:2,3 ————— A major decision

❏ I choose to teach this   Date Completed   _____
                                                      _____
                                                      _____

Sin + Time = Disaster

How often in Scripture, as well as our own lives, have we observed the principle that sin, if given time, spreads its painful consequences like a cancer. If left untreated, it will eventually kill the patient.

Look at the familiar story of David and Bathsheba. David's sin was bad enough and would have had consequences in any event. But he allowed time to pass without cleaning up his sin and the result was a disaster. Instead of adultery, which might have been forgiven with restitution, time allowed it to grow into murder, lying by someone with great responsibility, and last but not least, an example to David's family and the royal court that spawned havoc for a generation to come. Read the account in II Samuel 11-15. It could be the script for 6 months of daytime soaps.

Sin is like thorns. Given enough time, it will entangle and choke what might otherwise have been a fruitful life.

This is one of those principles that has a great visual example available for all of us to use with our kids. When summer is well along, be on the lookout for a place where thorns, scrub brush or other growth has over taken a vacant lot, a creek, or maybe your neighbor's lawn. Something that once was functional or beautiful but now it is neither functional nor beautiful. Take a few minutes to observe this on the way to another simple date night or an ice cream run. Then later, with your time together away from home, discuss David and Bathsheba**, the overgrown vacant lot, and what happens when we allow sin and time to mix together in our lives.

While no yard or vacant lot is beyond repair, discuss the amount of time and work that would be required to restore it to usefulness. The same is true for our lives.

** If you can think of an example closer to your kid's lives than David and Bathsheba, use it.

❏ I choose to teach this   Date Completed   _____

_____

_____

Assume You're Being Watched

There are two levels where this principle applies. The first is very simple. If you're ever tempted to think you're alone and away from home, family, parents or other believers, think again. We've all had it happen. You're on a business trip in some obscure town or airport half-way to Puca Puca and instead of being anonymous, you hear your name and it's your uncle Bob, or a couple from your Sunday School class or an unbeliever friend that knows you're a Christian. This applies to your kids too, when they might think they're out of yours and God's sight.

The second level is more daily. It applies consistently to our kids and us. When we claim Christ in front of the world (or even just a few neighbors or schoolmates) they will naturally observe our behavior to see if our walk matches our talk. You see, if we are inconsistent, claiming to follow Christ but routinely displaying a lack of integrity, then they can mentally let themselves off the hook, and for the time being conclude that Christianity is a fable for the benefit of those who want to soothe their fears of the afterlife. You and I, and our kids, don't have a choice. We represent Jesus Christ and all that He is once we are known as Christians. When you discuss this principle, be sure to acknowledge that we will all fail to some extent, sometime. But if that slip is in contrast to a general life of Christ-like love and integrity, your light will shine, though the world will likely never admit it to you.

As you think and talk about this, share an example from your own life where you learned that someone had made a special effort to covertly verify whether your actions matched your words.

❏ I choose to teach this   Date Completed   _____
                                                          _____
                                                          _____

Preparing and Sharing a Brief Personal Testimony of Faith in Christ

In the summer of 1975, I sold books door-to-door for the Southwestern Company of Nashville, Tennessee. That was a learning experience on many levels, as you might imagine. For 17 weeks, we sold books on a 100% commission basis, paying our own expenses. Part of Southwestern's 130-year history included bringing all of us untrained, inexperienced students, by the thousands into Nashville, TN for a week of sales training before we were ever allowed to approach the first doorstep. Most of that training consisted of memorizing a 10-12 minute presentation. We used to call it a "sales talk". Without that memorized preparation, college students would never have had the confidence and courage to approach complete strangers, dialog with them about the education of their children, and close a sale.

As Christians, I think there is a direct correlation. No we're not really "selling" anything. It is the Holy Spirit who convicts men and women of their sins and draws them to Himself. But He has given us the privilege of being part of the process. He asks us to, in effect, approach complete strangers, build relationships with them and dialog with them about something much more sensitive and threatening than books. We are to share with them God's love for sinners, His finished plan to save all who will accept Him and His righteous judgment on those who reject Him.

Is it any wonder that without a prepared "sales talk", we never seem to get around to sharing the Gospel? A three minute personal testimony is only a beginning, but if we can have our own personal story well prepared, almost memorized, it will roll off our lips at those times when God has prepared a friend or neighbor to hear of His love and salvation.

Make it a family project. Have fun with it. Role play teens with parents, mom with dad. Even younger children will gain great confidence in their own faith by being able to verbalize it.

P.S. As with everything else, dad, this will never happen unless you decide to give it a shot.

❏ I choose to teach this   Date Completed   _____

_____

_____

What is a Man in God's Design?

Our modern culture with its proud and arrogant independence from God has lost much of our understanding of God's original intended design. This is true for our understanding of the role of government, community, the church, the family and even how we perceive ourselves and our roles as men and women. Grade school students were surveyed a few years ago on current issues and role models. When asked whether Michael Jackson was a man or woman, a surprising percentage responded "both". When our sexuality is defined by our culture as a personal choice, is it any wonder that the result is confused, painful relationships and weak commitments?

So what is a man and what is a woman in God's original and perfect design?

Obviously, we can't develop this subject here, instead, let's look together at some key verses and principles of Scripture so that you can use them as the basis for a discussion with your kids. Perhaps more important than trying to achieve simple answers, the process of you as a father leading them through this discussion will bring positive results on many levels.

1. **Genesis 1:27 says: " So God created mankind in his own image...male and female he created them"** The sexes are clearly defined as different, unique from each other and intended so, as part of God's perfect design. How do you think God intended the sexes to be different and yet compliment each other?

2. **Genesis 1:27. "God blessed them and said 'Be fruitful and multiply in number'."** Sex and procreation is instituted here between husbands and wives.

3. **Genesis 2:15. "The Lord God took the man and put him in the garden to work it and take care of it."** Before sin entered the world, God gave man work to fill his time and consume his energies, and it was good. How does our work, in itself, please God?

4. **Genesis 2:18. "And God said, 'It is not good for the man to be alone. I will make a helper suitable for him."** Man was incomplete and apparently incapable of reaching his full potential alone. So God made woman to complete and balance him. The

term "husband", on the other hand, means "a caretaker, one who protects and nurtures" in this case his wife.

Throughout the New Testament, Scripture uses the illustration of Christ in the male role of bridegroom and the Church in the female role of bride. For this, we should not conclude superiority of men over women, but rather that God's original design for a man is to be the leader, initiator, protector, and provider just as Christ is for the Church. Were it not so, Scripture might have used other relationships to make the point. When you consider the agenda that militant feminists have to redefine your daughter's and your son's concept of men and women, don't just leave this subject unspoken. Discuss it, even though your life and your wife's will speak louder still.

❑ I choose to teach this   Date Completed   _____

_____

_____

What is a Woman In God's Design?

Continuing from the previous discussion of God's design for men, here are some Biblical references and principles that help us understand God's design for women. Let me encourage you to discuss both sexes even if you have only boys or only girls. A discussion of the opposite sex is equally important as their own.

1. Referring to women in the early church, **1 Peter 3:3ff says: "Your beauty should not come from outward adornment such as braided hair or the wearing of gold jewelry and fine clothes. Instead it should be that of your inner self, the unfading beauty of a gentle and quiet spirit which is of great worth in God's sight."**

Do you think Peter is teaching that women should have no concern of their outward beauty? What standard must young women use to judge their own value or acceptability? How should a Christian woman's sense of self worth and value differ from the world's view of women?

2. 1 John 2:15-17 says: **"Do not love the world or anything in the world. If anyone loves the world, the love of the Father is not in him. For everything in the world – the cravings of sinful man, the lust of his eyes and the boasting of what he has and does—comes not from the Father but from the world. The world and its desires pass away, but the man who does the will of God lives forever."**

The three desires in verse 16 can be loosely paraphrased as "I want to do, I want to have, and I want to be."

How do women, from the world's perspective, fit into these verses? If the world, and women in particular, accept this standard for themselves, what does v. 17 tell us about God's design for women?

In these discussions on God's design for men and women, we've intentionally left the much larger subjects of husband/wife and mother/father for another day. In a conversation with your kids try to limit the scope to men and women in God's sight. It may be easy to fall into the more familiar teachings on spouses and parents, but for the time being neither of those apply to your kids. More important for them is an acceptance of a sovereign God who made men and women different, equally valuable, and designed to work together in harmony.

❏ I choose to teach this   Date Completed   _____

_____

_____

"But Dad, I'm in Love"

We would all like to believe that our own marriage is example enough to provide our kids with a realistic model when they begin considering marriage for themselves. Look outside of your own four walls, however, and you'll conclude that a silent example is not enough. As responsible dads, we can't let the world define marital love for our kids. We give our kids direct guidance on choosing a car, choosing friends, choosing a college and none of these are in the same league for the importance and life-long consequences of choosing a mate. Once our son or daughter finds themselves hopelessly infatuated and old enough to act on those feelings, it is an uphill battle to only then discuss what marital love really is.

For those of us who have experienced marriage for many years, we've come to know the meaning of commitment, self-sacrifice, the joy of shared ideals, of love. Most of us would agree that when we first met our wives, the strong feeling of attraction bore little resemblance to real love that stands the test of time.

Love is commitment backed up by personal character that can deliver over a lifetime of good and bad times. An 18 year old experiencing strong feelings for someone may be very sincere, and it is a new experience for them, but we must be the anchor to convince them that this alone is not love.

Here are a few discussion starters rooted in the Bible's definition of love in I Corinthians 13 and Ephesians 5.

(please turn the page)

What love is	What love is not
Patient – willing to grow through a sustained courtship.	Self-seeking – would a marriage now, with all of its life changing responsibilities be the best for my sweetheart?
Endures all things – growing into a mature relationship takes time.	Sudden, warm feelings of attraction—there is no such thing as falling in love in one night or even a few days.
Full appreciation of self sacrifice – do I fully understand the life changing responsibilities that await me?	
Willing and able to build a household independent of parents.	
Willing to accept an entirely new role of leadership, self sacrifice, submission, and shared responsibility.	

Have this conversation with your 17-year-old before they tell you they're in love and you find yourself on the defensive at a time when their emotions can out-weigh your experience.

❏ I choose to teach this   Date Completed   _____

_____

_____

What is Your World View?

Do you know what your worldview is? Can you explain it? More important to our subject here, does your 17-year-old know? Unless we have some level of understanding in this area, it is a certainty that our teenagers will leave home unprepared for the very convincing, complete systems of thought that will hit them primarily in the college environment.

Our worldview is that set of overall, foundational beliefs that drive our more specific opinions and actions. Do you believe in God and some final standard of right and wrong? Then you have a Biblical Judeo/Christian worldview whether you know it or not. Are you an atheist who believes that ethics are purely a matter of relative good or evil depending on the circumstances? If so, you hold a secular humanist worldview. Actually, there are four primary worldviews in western culture and those who strongly hold and advocate them are as zealous for their ideas as any Christian missionary. It is not simply a matter of intellectuals who wish to rebel against and pick apart Christianity. No, our colleges are filled with intellectuals who will bury the unprepared freshman with clearly articulated, consistent philosophies in subjects like the basis for law, the origin of man, man's worth or lack of it, the ultimate goal of civil government, the possibility of any divine intervention and a hundred others.

Several years ago, I heard a Christian student comment that his first few weeks at college raised a pile of questions and issues he'd never heard of in Sunday School. We might be tempted to laugh, but if it were our own son or daughter, we might wish we could go back only a year or two and work through these issues so at least it doesn't come as a shocking surprise that there are well constructed, thoughtful challenges to everything our kids assumed to be true.

One book that clearly lays out the four Western worldviews and their implications for all areas of culture is "Understanding the Times" by David A. Nobel, pub. Summit Ministries, 1995. A summary chart of the four worldviews is shown on the next page. (Used by permission) Another modern classic on the subject is "How Now Shall We Live", by Charles Colson.

None of us need to be philosophers, but we must see the danger and risks if our seniors graduate and we send them off to college without any preparation for the intellectual bushwhacking they will experience.

❏ I choose to teach this   Date Completed   _____

_____

_____

FOUR WESTERN WORLDVIEW MODELS

SOURCES	SECULAR HUMANISM — HUMANIST MANIFESTOS I AND II	MARXISM/LENINNISM — WRITINGS OF MARX AND LENIN	COSMIC HUMANISM — WRITINGS OF SPANGLER, FERGUSON, ETC.	BIBLICAL CHRISTIANITY — BIBLE
THEOLOGY	Atheism	Atheism	Pantheism	Theism
PHILOSOPHY	Naturalism	Dialectical Materialism	Non-Naturalism	Supernaturalism
ETHICS	Relativism	Proletariat Morality	Relativism	Absolutes
BIOLOGY	Darwinian Evolution	Darwinian/Punctuated Evolution	Darwinian/Punctuated Evolution	Creation
PSYCHOLOGY	Self-Actualization	Behaviorism	Collective Consciousness	Mind/Body
SOCIOLOGY	Non-Traditional Family	Abolition of Home, Church and State	Non-Traditional Home, Church and State	Traditional Home, Church and State
LAW	Positive Law	Positive Law	Self-Law	Biblical and Natural Law
POLITICS	World Government (Globalism)	New World Order (New Civilization)	New Age Order	Justice, Freedom and Order
ECONOMICS	Socialism	Socialism	Universal Enlightened Production	Stewardship of Property
HISTORY	Historical Evolution	Historical Materialism	Evolutionary Godhood	Historical Resurrection

Accountability for All Age Levels

In the acknowledgements of this book I credit my Basic Accountability Group (BAG) as the seed bed for many of the ideas shared here. An accountability group is not a novel idea only for men with school age children. This concept may have been expanded, most notably for men, in the last 20 years, but the need for accountability is as old as the battle over obedience and sin.

Warren Wiersbe, the author, radio Bible teacher and pastor of Moody Church has said, "Men [and women] never dive into sin, they always wade in." The wading may end in a final lunge, but there are always opportunities to pull back when we are ankle or knee deep. That's where accountability must be the life preserver that prevents a spiritual casualty and avoids untold pain and long term consequences.

Several years ago a dear friend who had been a spiritual mentor to me acknowledged that he "waded in up to his knees" by allowing a relationship with another woman get too close. In the following months, it became clear that he had, in fact, committed adultery. My purpose in mentioning it here is to see the other side of the coin. Had that man been part of an accountability relationship where lives were frequently and confidently measured against God's standard, the outcome would have almost certainly been different. I can assure you, no one would have been more eager to rewrite history than that young man.

When our children live at home, they are automatically accountable to us as dads. But do we have the courage to take that role and actually make it part of our interactions with them? Let me challenge you to move from childhood discipline to adolescent accountability with mutually agreed consequences for their actions. Matter of fact discussion of this principle as a life long need for men, women, grandparents, dads, moms, and teens will help set the stage that this is not a one way street mainly designed to control teenagers. Rather, it is something they should seek out and continue through their adult years. And, like anything else, it will be much easier for your kids to accept if they see an accountability group as a practical reality in your life long before you apply it to theirs.

❏ I choose to teach this   Date Completed   _____
_____
_____

55

Hedges and How to Use Them

Hedges are useful and beautiful things that can enhance the value of our property in many ways. A hedge can be used to divide one property from another. It can be used to cover over or keep some unsightly part of your property out of view. It can also be a barrier for safety reasons. All of these practical definitions also apply when we think of hedges in a spiritual context. Spiritually speaking, a hedge is when you and I intentionally set up a barrier to prevent us from going near, seeing, hearing, or in some other way experiencing something, which too often leads into sin.

For example, if pornography is the thing to be avoided, it's probably not enough to say, "I won't look at any of those filthy magazines." A hedge is saying, "I will not go into 7-11 or the hotel gift shop, alone, ever." That creates a barrier so you aren't faced with the temptation and opportunity to look at those magazines. **A hedge is a practical boundary you can set for yourself for the intentional purpose of preventing you from being in a position to commit the sin you want to avoid.**

In I Cor. 10:13, God says: "No temptation has seized you except what is common to man. And God is faithful, He will not let you be tempted beyond what you can bear. But when you are tempted He will also provide a way out so you can stand up under it." More directly to the point of hedges, Romans 13:14 says "…and make no provision to satisfy the sinful desires of the flesh."

The concept is simple but very effective when it is put into practice. Discuss the concept with your 12 or 13 year old when you see an illustration of it. The opportunities to build spiritual hedges will start in their teen years. Then, when they leave home, this simple tool for overcoming temptation will already be very familiar. For an in-depth study, look for Hedges, by Jerry Jenkins, Moody Press.

❏ I choose to teach this   Date Completed   _____

_____

_____

General Principles

Teach a child to choose the right path,
and when he is old, he will remain upon it.
Proverbs 22:6

The A T S Principle

Once there were three men, in fact, they were your friends. One was a neighbor, one was a friend at your church and the third was a supplier to your company. All three were capable and for the most part responsible men, but only one followed and reaped the rewards of the ATS principle.

The first man, your neighbor, promised to help you put up your garage door opener last Saturday. But just when you got to the part that was a two-man job, he couldn't be found, so as of today, you're still getting out of your car in the rain.

The second man agreed to show up at church to help build the sets for the children's program. You didn't have a chance to connect for several weeks beforehand, but on the agreed day, there he was ready to go. He delivered exactly as promised. It's good he was there, but no one noticed much. After all, there were six other guys too and they all did what they promised.

But the third man, your supplier at work, demonstrated the ATS principle. He delivered his services on time, with the expected quality. But when the invoice came it was for $1,000 less than the contracted amount, so you called to ask why. He only replied that their costs had come in lower than expected and he was able to pass along part of the savings to you. Now there is a man you can sail in a storm with. There is a man you'll not soon forget. In fact, the loyalty created by his actions will almost certainly reward him many times over. This man displayed the ATS principle. He gave what was expected <u>A</u>nd <u>T</u>hen <u>S</u>ome.

Delivering at 100% is usually good enough to keep you off the hot seat. For the most part it goes unnoticed. But deliver at 105% of anyone's expectations and you're an absolute hero. Loyalty is created, friendships deepen and you are often rewarded in both practical and intangible ways.

❏ I choose to teach this   Date Completed   _____
                                                          _____
                                                          _____

It's Not the Will to Win, It's the Will to Prepare to Win

During the 1996 Summer Olympics, one athlete's personal story stood out from most others. It was the story of a truly amateur athlete on the U. S. team. No dream team here. No world-class sprinter with genes that God actually intended for a gazelle. No, just an average human resources manager and mother of three who happened to get up at 5:00 a.m. to shoot 175 arrows before breakfast and another 175 after work.

Hers is a sport that most of us can relate to. Most of life, in fact, is not won by the dream team. To be sure, there are so few dream teamers that they're only useful as a spectator sport for the rest of us. In the real world of homes, offices, job sites and families, it's all guys like you and me. We are the contestants and there are no dream teamers in this league. The good news for all of us is that, as a general rule, we can <u>choose</u> to win or at least compete at a very superior level. The bad news is that it takes indescribable discipline in those private moments and quiet hours when there is no one cheering us on, no one even noticing that we are preparing to win.

Look around you. Did the pianist sit down one day and play to the applause of the audience? Did the executive who gave the keynote address at your trade show get there because he won the lottery? And the father who sees his son leave for college with growing maturity and a healthy confidence in God and himself – does that happen because father and son had a talk the night before he left? In our league where there are no dream teamers, it's all in the will to <u>prepare</u> to win. Winning, whatever form that may take for you, is the natural and sure result for the man or child who is willing to <u>prepare</u> to win.

Let me encourage you to have a heart to heart, one on one discussion, at the teachable moment when you son or daughter is struck with admiration for someone whose visible results are proof of his or her invisible preparation.

❏ I choose to teach this   Date Completed   _____

_____

_____

When In Doubt, Don't Speak Out

How often have we all looked back on an experience where we kept talking, raised a question, or otherwise blurted out our thoughts before giving them any consideration. Oh, once in a great while we'll wish we had said more, but in my case, the problem is usually that it seemed important or funny at the time, but it just didn't seem that insightful or important once it had crossed my lips.

Nine times out of ten, we'll be glad we said less when we're uncertain about the value or the impression our words will leave. James 3:6 calls the tongue a deadly poison, harder to control than the rest of the body, so it's good self discipline to learn to say less than everything that comes to mind.

On a positive note, Proverbs 17:20 says, "Even a fool is thought wise if he keeps silent, and discerning if he holds his tongue." After you discuss this principle, be alert and commend your son or daughter when you see even the smallest evidence of them holding their tongue, when it would have been the easy and natural thing to blurt out their thoughts.

❏ I choose to teach this   Date Completed   _____
                                                     _____
                                                     _____

The Family Reading Program

Let's ask ourselves a question. In the 18+ years that our son or daughter is at home, is there time for them to read one book (outside of school) and make a brief report to the family? Of course, in 18 years, the answer is yes. Next question: Is there at least one book that is very important and valuable that you would prescribe for that one report to the family? Most certainly, yes again.

Now these were easy questions when you consider a span of 18 years, and by now, you can guess where I am going. In 18 years, is there time for two books reports? – Yes. Three? – Yes. Well then, how many? It's up to you, but I would challenge you to make a series of book reports the prerequisite for an important, long term goal of your son or daughter. Make it age appropriate, of course. The size of the task and weight of the material must be appropriate to the size and weight of the child.

Just think for a moment with me. How much would you be willing to pay for your 16-year-old to be highly motivated to read, think through and report on "The Training of the Twelve" the classic book by F.F. Bruce on how Jesus influenced and trained the 12 disciples? Or try "The Knowledge of the Holy" by A.W. Tozer. Or "The Cost of Discipleship" by Bonnhoeffer. You pick the titles, but when the reward is high in the eyes of your child, they'll devour the book. In terms of the lifelong impact it can have on your teenager, if you're like me, you'll be willing to tie this to some pretty significant rewards.

If you have the privilege of beginning the process while your kids are still in grade school, it will become familiar to them early on. By the time they are teenagers, the basic contract will be accepted, only the book titles and the rewards will be up for discussion. You might even be surprised when they suggest it to you as a means to their objectives. Remember, you hold the deciding vote on which and how many titles get tied to a particular objective, but once agreed, don't even think of backing out. The standard you set for their written/oral report, demonstrated by your time and undivided attention has everything to do with how serious they take it. Set the time frame together and then don't deviate from it. Help them if they need it, work together if it will draw them in, but never transfer the weight of the project from them.

Their insight in a book report will be valuable now and priceless to both of you in the future.

It is hard to narrow down a list from hundreds of worthwhile books, but here are some of the titles that made it to our boys' reading list.

Holy Heroes Book Pack – Family Life – age 8+
The Chronicles of Narnia – C.S. Lewis – age 10+
The Book of Virtues – Bennett – age 10+
The Biography of Abraham Lincoln (100-200 selected pages) age 12+
Answers to Tough Questions – McDowell – age 14+
Life on the Edge – Dobson – age14+
Pure Excitement – White – age 15+
Mere Christianity – Lewis – age 16+
Seven Habits – Covey – age 17+
Understanding the Times – Nobel – age 17+ (abridged)
The Cost of Discipleship – Bonnhoeffer – age 18+
The Training of Twelve – Bruce – age 18+
How Now Shall We Live – Colson – age 18+
Total Truth – Pearcey – age 18+
The Knowledge of the Holy – Tozer – age 18 +
Fit to be Tied – Hybels – age 18+ (pre-marriage)

Most of these titles could be found at a good bookstore. For those that are out of print, they'll know how to get them.

❑ I choose to teach this   Date Completed   _____
                                                     _____
                                                     _____

The Trees and Forests Principle

When I was 12, our family moved to Wichita, Kansas. Being the son of the church's only pastor had its advantages and its drawbacks. One of those (I'm not sure which) came into play when a church member named Jim asked my dad if I'd be interested in a brief summer job helping to landscape his ranch house. My first assignment was to pick up all the small stones in what was to become the front lawn. Not a huge job, but surely a frustrating one. Like many projects we all face, it was hard to know where to begin. I wandered around the lawn picking up small stones, but everywhere I looked, there were more. I simply couldn't address the whole lawn at once. After a short time, Jim realized this task took more patience and focus than I had so we ran an errand for the rest of the afternoon. I didn't know it then, but that was an example of the trees and forests principle.

Here's how it goes: If you or I were asked to cut down a forest, it would be understood that there is only one way to do it – one tree at a time. Imagine literally trying to cut down a "forest". You might put large engines mounted on a flatbed truck, each driving a chainsaw type apparatus several hundred feet long. Then drive slowly and cut the whole forest…. well, it's ridiculous. There are not tools designed to cut "forests". Just like there is no way for you or me to successfully manage a two-year product launch, or for our six year old to clean his room. The job is overwhelming when viewed as a whole. But when the forest is viewed one tree at a time—when the product launch is broken into recognizable, achievable tasks—then we know where to begin and the paralysis is broken.

I might have finished that yard back in 1968 if Jim had taken two pieces of string and created a 3-foot wide section of lawn. As a 12 year old, I could have handled a 3'x30' strip picking up every stone, then repeating the process 3 feet over. It was the whole yard that was overwhelming.

My boys and I talked about this when they were 6 and 9 years old. I can remember it well because no one was more surprised than I, when several weeks later we asked them to pick up the playroom. I came in to find them making steady progress and Colson announced, "Look Dad, trees and forests."

It is not a substitute for motivation, but when a task seems overwhelming, this simple principle still applies whether our kids are 6, 16, or 36.

❑ I choose to teach this　　　Date Completed　　　_____

_____

_____

You Can't Get a Hit if You Never Step Up to the Plate

This principle seems straight forward enough. So why is it that you and I, and our fathers before us, often spend more time in the bleachers of life while others are getting hits at the plate? Let me share a few reasons that I hope will motivate us, and our kids after us, to be hitters whenever the opportunity arises.

1. The biggest factor is surely negative inertia. We're stuck on our own self-perceptions, believing that unless we've done this before, it's not realistic to try now. Getting started really is more than half the battle.

2. We assume that this opportunity is so new and outside of our experience that we would surely strike out even if we did venture up to the plate. Wrong. You have skills, I have common sense, our kids have abilities that often will produce a hit.

3. We think we'll wait for a better opportunity, or a better fit to come along. The implication in this thinking is that there is a very limited number of opportunities and if we waste our effort here, we won't be available or we'll, for some reason, be disqualified for a "much better" opportunity. The opposite is actually true. Opportunities seem to line up for the person who is willing to take an honest shot at it. And if you miss badly, it's not a disqualification for the next pitch.

4. Embarrassment. We're all reluctant to step out in front of the stadium of life and face pitches that may be fast and hard. But ask yourself, did the person you're visualizing in your mind right now always get hits – even at first? And when he missed, did you think less of him? No, a man of character and courage who misses, and maybe even strikes out, receives your quiet admiration and respect.

Teddy Roosevelt said it best:
"The credit belongs to the man who is actually in the arena, who strives valiantly, who knows the great enthusiasms, the great devotions, and

spends himself in a worthy cause, who at the best, knows the triumph of high achievement, and who, at the worst, if he fails, at least fails while daring greatly, so that his place will never be with those cold and timid souls who know neither victory nor defeat."

I suggest you wait until your son or daughter has had even a small hit at the plate of life. Just so long as it is a victory in their eyes. Then in less than 24 hours, have a date night and share with them how great a principle they just demonstrated.

❑ I choose to teach this   Date Completed   _____

_____

_____

Horns, and When to Toot Yours

Think for a moment. Try to picture someone in your mind—someone who represents the most competent, mature, disciplined and respected person you know. When was the last time you heard that person talking about his own accomplishment? Probably never. In fact, it's hard to imagine that person attempting to convince others of their personal value. Why? Because they don't need to. Everyone (including themselves) is already convinced of his or her personal value, accomplishment or skills.

What most of us don't realize is that "tooting your own horn" reduces your self-esteem and the respect you receive from others, while holding your tongue when given an obvious opportunity to speak about yourself, increases the respect from others. At that moment, an interesting thing often happens. Our silence creates an opening that someone else fills with words of praise and credit for us. Those words have a powerful and positive effect, but if <u>we</u> had said the same thing, it would have had an equally powerful negative effect.

Even if you're not the most respected, disciplined person in the eyes of yourself and others, all the more reason not to toot your own horn. It only drives down your personal esteem in the eyes of others.

Proverbs 27:2 says it plain and clear. "Let another man praise you and not your own mouth, someone else and not your own lips."

Wait for a positive or negative example of this that is observed by your pre-teenager, then have an ice cream and discuss positive and negative examples where people they know toot their own horn or wait for others to do it.

❏ I choose to teach this   Date Completed   _____
                                                       _____
                                                       _____

Telling the Truth Especially When it Requires Courage

On the surface, this may seem so obvious as not to merit any discussion here. But let's pursue it for a moment. Have you taken the time to really talk with your kids about the reason behind this most obvious virtue?

Like most things in life, lessons learned in adulthood come at a much higher cost and more painfully than if we learn the pattern right as children.

Telling the truth when the stakes are low is not an issue. The real challenge involves the courage to tell the truth when it will surely bring anger, discomfort and all kinds of teeth gnashing from others. Making mistakes is human, and usually, easily forgotten. But a mistake hidden by lies is cause for the most serious consequences in the adult realm, perhaps the worst being the sure loss of our credibility and reputation. Conversely, someone who has the courage to come clean to his own hurt, usually gains respect in the long run.

As a father, you're well aware of this, but the key to transmitting this to our kids is a relentless insistence on full disclosure now, even though the childish consequences wouldn't seem to merit so much attention. Avoiding the adult consequences depends on how you set their pattern now.

Some years ago I worked with a company that had a philosophy as part of our overall Quality Advantage Program. It said: "It's easy to succeed if it's OK to fail." The principle was that "telling the truth as soon as you uncover your mistake saves untold problems for everyone and, in fact, demonstrates your own character." A mistake or even a willful act that is repented of early is usually manageable, but the longer it is concealed the more combustion when it finally does come to light. In our printing and mailing business we would say: "A mistake corrected early may cost a few dollars, if it goes to press it will cost thousands, but if it goes in the mail, it will cost millions."

Still, how many of us continue to fail at this most basic principle well into adulthood. The thought is that this time, just this once, we won't be found out. But with each passing day that we don't come clean, it only intensifies the consequences when we are finally exposed.

Tell the truth early for two reasons:

1. It demonstrates your character and courage now, and

2. It allows you to escape with much lighter consequences.

As a father I've tried to reward the courage when transgressions are admitted early and freely, but also determined to discipline the concealed lies, knowing that if they learn a few painful lessons now, it will surely save them the immensely more painful experiences that will touch them as adults.

Dads: Perhaps more than any other principle in this book, if our kids don't have this resolved in their own experience, before they leave home, it has the potential for life altering failure in the adult realm. Just look at the corporate world or Washington, D.C. if you need to be convinced.

❏ I choose to teach this   Date Completed   _____
                                                     _____
                                                     _____

Burning Bridges

Several years ago, Lora Sue and I had just started attending a new church after moving to the area. They must have been short on music one Sunday because we were asked to sing. Since we didn't know any accompanist, we thought it easiest to use a tape-recorded accompaniment track. There we were in front of a full church of strangers. The soundman pushed the button but nothing happened. He tried again, and again, and nothing. We had carefully cued up the sound track but after 30 or 45 seconds of dead silence, I began talking. I don't really remember about what— – it was sort of a near death experience. If it had been some anonymous group of strangers we might never have returned, but we were committed to being a part of that church for years to come. I spent the remainder of the service planning how to express my true feelings to the soundman. But, when the time came, whether for cowardice or good sense I don't know, I thanked him for his efforts.

How often has this happened to all of us? You are thoroughly aggravated by the actions or words of a stranger or new acquaintance, but thanks to some distant training in patience and good manners, you avoid verbally taking their head off and instead, hold your tongue. The principle of burning bridges only comes to mind two weeks later when you meet that person again, but this time it's to ask if they would please be one of the 14 people you promised to recruit for the school carnival.

The principle is simple, but many of us can also tell stories from the other side of the coin where we should have known better, but went ahead with a full napalm attack on some poor "bridge". Then, as life tends to do, our path comes around and we really need to cross that bridge again. We lose badly either way at that point. 1. Either the person points out that their "bridge" is too damaged to cross or, 2. they graciously allow us to cross and we rightly feel like an immature adolescent who got caught in his folly.

Let me try to take this one step further. God has allowed all of us to have work partners, neighbors, or volunteers at church that all too often aggravate us to exhaustion. They may be weak or without vision, but God is not, and He is constantly taking broken, imperfect vessels like you and me, and building something wonderful. Only a fool destroys the bricks and tools he has been given and then wonders why his wall is so small.

Don't burn the bridges God puts in your path. It serves no useful purpose for you or Him.

☐ I choose to teach this   Date Completed   _____

_____

_____

The Hired Hand Principle

(No one cares about your business as much as you do———don't expect them to.)

Several years ago, I joined together with six other neighbor families to share the cost of a community well, which would improve the water quality in each of our homes. One neighbor was a lawyer so he drew up a simple document we all signed relating to the cost and maintenance. Another took the task of overseeing the backhoe operator who would lay the 1 ½ inch pipe from the well to each of our homes. Each of us was in for several thousand dollars, so I assumed careful attention was being paid to our plat of surveys and the location of our specific septic fields in particular. I came home from work one afternoon to find a two foot wide, six foot deep trench running the length of my back yard up to the designated point on the house. This was expected, except for the fact that the trench had cut right through our septic field. The health department promptly said a water line could never go through a septic field, so the trench was re-routed to the house. Just try to imagine a six-foot mole going through your favorite putting green and you begin to get the picture.

The result was that I had a damaged or ruined septic field, and a big, expensive mess. I had assumed my neighbor would be diligent to avoid all our septic fields, after all, he had made sure to avoid <u>his</u> own septic field.

In John 10, Jesus tells how the hired hand would save his own skin but let all the sheep perish when danger comes. It's because the hired hand doesn't have ownership of the sheep. Learn the lesson. You have only yourself to blame if you assume that an outsider has the same motivations as you when it comes to your work, your family, your finances, your life.

❏ I choose to teach this   Date Completed   _____

_____

_____

The Train Tracks Principle

(Reductio ad absurdum logic in practical terms)

For this principle, let's assume that train rails are two perfectly straight lines. If you were building the train tracks, you'd lay each of the two tracks down and they might appear to be parallel. Going out five or ten feet, they might still appear to be parallel. But go out half a mile and the true picture will be very evident—whether they're coming together or going apart.

This principle can help our kids determine the truth whether it's a math problem or political issue. **Take the key issues or variables, extend them out to the extreme, and a much clearer picture usually emerges.**

Let me offer a simple example. A few years back I was buying a set of car tires. The store carried two brands that were equal in quality and price. I wanted the widest tread I could get, however. Standing them side-by-side, it was hard to tell since the tread pattern was different. But extending out the factors made the choice clear. I stacked up 4 tires of each brand. It was clear—the one stack was 2" taller – easy decision.

Consider another application of the train tracks principle with more complex factors – the abortion issue. I personally feel strongly about the sanctity of human life, but don't misunderstand. My purpose here is not, in a few paragraphs, to attempt a thorough discussion of this issue. Instead, because the issues and arguments used by both camps are familiar to most of us, let it serve as a good example of the train tracks logic.

Is a human baby alive and deserving of protection two weeks after birth? Yes. Follow the train tracks a little in one direction. Is the baby worthy three weeks earlier?

This logic would require a yes since that same baby could have been delivered 3 weeks preterm and we'd be looking at a post-birth baby. Well, go further down the tracks. Is there any point at which the fetus is fundamentally different in terms of its 46 chromosomes and unique identity from the mother?

Now, let's run the logic the other way. Let's assume a pro-choice position and test its validity with the train tracks principle. If it is OK to abort a fetus two weeks after conception, is it OK at three months? How about nine months? How about nine months after birth? Remember the key here is holding all factors constant. At all four of these points the main factors

73

are that the baby is a unique individual, complete in its human makeup and totally <u>dependent</u> on external care to prevent death in a few hours or days.

The constant factors are the straight, unbending rails. It's only by going some distances in one direction or the other (in this case earlier or later term) that the implications of our thinking (in this case the morality of aborting a fetus) become painfully clear.

I hope you can see past my choice of subject here. The purpose is not to convince you or your kids on the morality of abortion. But as you and your kids contemplate this and a hundred greater or lessor issues, give them the train tracks principle as a useful tool in their thought process.

❏ I choose to teach this   Date Completed   _____

_____

_____

Pornography is a Progressive, Ugly Trap

Soft porn is only a stepping stone and a slippery slope to more destructive themes. Allowing yourself to be touched by this poison in the guise of "finding out about it" is akin to walking, by choice, through an Indiana Jones snake pit just to "find out" how poisonous they are.

Don't leave your early teenage boys defenseless to learn these lessons alone. If you do, statistics indicate that some of our boys will learn long and painful lessons in this area, and those they love, including you, will be entangled by the results.

When your boys are 35, let them reflect back with gratitude on a dad who had the courage to teach and model these lessons forthrightly. Here are a couple ideas for dealing with your own boys:

1. Fire in the fireplace is a warm and beautiful thing. But pull that same fire out into the family room and it becomes a costly and painful disaster. Explain the same is true for how God made us to enjoy the beauty and sexuality of our wives. Any other indulgence is a "fire in the family room."

2. Consider taking a Playboy with your pre-teenage son, privately, and say you're going to have a man-to-man talk. I'd leave it closed, but just having it there will create a strangely chilling effect on the allure of that stuff. Explain that these pictures are airbrushed fakes. The real girls have pimples and wrinkles just like real life. More importantly, the real girls are someone's daughters and sisters, many of whom would like to get away from that ugly business if they could.

When Graham and I had this talk, we even went so far as agreeing on what he would say and how he would handle it when some group of boys someday got a hold of some pornography. Because of the anti-drug education, he understood the concept of addiction so we agreed on these exact words. He would tell other boys: "That stuff is dirty and addictive." Then he would leave. No hesitation or looking back for their reactions—just leave. Day or night. Pick your own words if you prefer, but role play this together. You be the other boys. Poke fun at the "sissy" who won't be a part of this so that your son is familiar, hardened and resolved before the future event ever occurs. Then, in the heat of the moment, his decision and his words will be firm. It's not a question of if, but when he comes home someday, and tells you how this played out in real life, it will be a moment of joy and connection for both of you.

Dad, it goes without saying that your own house must be in order here. If you don't have integrity on this one, imagine answering your son's questions when he asks how you learned to stay away from pornography.

❏ I choose to teach this   Date Completed   _____

_____

_____

The Short Cut Principle (The Ends and Means Problem).

Throughout Scripture there are examples of fathers and other leaders, who knew the right things to do, and in some cases had even received promises from God for a particular outcome. But, as the months turned into years, or other circumstances converged to create a pressure situation for them, they convinced themselves that the noble and desired end justified all kinds of short cuts and violations of proven principles in order to get through the immediate problem.

It's amazing how a father's courageous action, clearly rooted in principle, becomes even more respectable when the intense light of a pressure situation is shined upon it. The very pressures that tempt you to take a short cut will often cause people and circumstances to come together in a win-win compromise. This is the human perspective, not to mention God's supernatural intervention and protection on his children when they act in faith, staying the course and refusing to take the short cut opportunity.

Abraham was 75 years old when God promised to make his descendants a great nation. Some 10 years passed but there was no son and he became convinced that Sarah's age was the irreversible problem. In spite of God's explicit promise, he took the short cut in order to help God along. He had relations with his household servant girl, Hagar. Imagine the pain, embarrassment and regret some 15 years later when the real son of the promise, Isaac, was born to – you guessed it – Sarah.

God doesn't need our help. He's given us clear principles to live by. Show your kids this story from Genesis 12 and look for modern life examples whenever you're faced with an opportunity to take a short cut.

❏ I choose to teach this   Date Completed   _____
                                                 _____
                                                 _____

77

Trips, Rewards and Ceremonies

During an entire childhood we have the opportunity to build a few, very special events—so special that they can create shared memories and help to anchor your relationship for the predicted storms of the teen-age years. Too many events, of course, would create inflation and the value and memory of each would be lost. Here is the short list of the significant, planned events that occurred in our home.

The 10-year-old business trip

Even if your career doesn't normally involve business travel, find a way to make this the one business trip you're sure to take. With weeks of advance planning and hype to your 10-year-old, pull them out of school to join you on a legitimate business trip. You can't do this with your customers more than once, but for one time, your customers will love this. They'll give you company trinkets and your son/daughter will learn more than they ever would in two days of school. Work with their school teacher in advance so that a small oral report to the class is required upon your return, explaining their dad's job and the things they learned about his work.

Be sure <u>both</u> of you wear a coat and tie for these appointments if that is at all appropriate to the work environment. This will further dignify the experience in the eyes of your young partner and of your clients. The time on the airplane and in business hotels with you will make an impression never to be forgotten. You'll be the recipient of free desserts and other special treatment. Nothing turns heads like walking into a restaurant with a 10-year-old in a sharp sport coat and tie, or dress and proper heels. (And be sure to take pictures for mom).

Reading the Bible through

At about age 12 (6th grade), your son or daughter should be ready to read the entire Bible through in a single year. (There are several printed schedules available to prescribe the daily reading.) Agree together that if this challenge is met, there will be a special trip as a reward. Choose together, but at the completion of this challenge, be sure you get on an airplane and go to an unfamiliar city for a favorite experience. In our house, it was a golf trip to Phoenix. With advance planning and effort, you can do this on a modest budget, but whatever you can afford to spend, it may be the most worthwhile investment you ever make.

During the year-long reading effort, periodically go to Sunday lunch—just you and your son/daughter—for a discussion of what they've read in the past couple months. Then at the end of the year, you're in for a most wonderful experience. Have a final Sunday lunch together and let your child give you an open-book report on the entire Bible. Sure it will be at a 6th grade level, but allow them the pride of demonstrating their learning from this long-term effort. Discuss some of the more interesting stories and the truths behind them. Then pack your bags and be sure the trip happens soon enough so that a 13-year-old connects it to the effort.

The Purity Ring

The summer before your child enters 9th grade, ask them if they will make a life size commitment to you and to God. Ask them if they will commit to sexual purity until they marry and to wear a ring symbolizing that commitment. Then go to a jewelry store or a favorite bookstore together and let them pick the simple band that they will wear for years to come.

I have seen this become the basis for a precious moment at wedding ceremonies/receptions where a young bride or groom will remove the ring they have been wearing for 10 years and give it to their spouse or perhaps a younger brother or sister coming up behind them. The symbol is obvious and the power of that moment is immense.

The 16-year-old challenge

You know the statistics for teen-age drivers. The likelihood of your 16-year-old son/daughter getting a ticket or being involved in an accident is high. Driver's ed. classes are important, but how can you ever motivate a 16-year-old male, brimming full of testosterone, or a young lady with cell phone in hand, to drive safely? In our house we agreed on two things:

1. If they had a ticket or accident, they would pay that ticket and the significantly increased insurance cost. (The ticket might be $75 but the insurance could go from the $400 they are already paying to over $800 every six months.)

2. If they went an entire year (to their 17th birthday) with no tickets or accidents, there would be a significant reward.

I can't guarantee your results, but praise God, in our house it worked. Both boys made it to their 17th birthday resulting in a private airplane flying lesson and a very fast racing boat ride on Lake Michigan. (Lora Sue will never know how fast.)

The 17-year-old road trip

Once your teen has been driving for a year, between school and friends, you may feel like you never see them. So talk about it for years in advance, that at age 17, you'll do a road trip together. Same formula—agree together on their favorite experience (golf, shopping, etc.) and then drive at least 600 miles to find it. It doesn't need to be extravagant. Maybe you'll camp if that is your style, but spend at least four days and three nights on a trip they'll never forget. And of course, they'll need to do some of the driving.

The 18-year-old ceremony

Following their 18th birthday, both you and your child will see the finish line coming very soon—where they leave home in some form. You will have invested days, years, some tears and maybe a few gray hairs at this point. Your son or daughter will know about the Circles of Responsibility, the ATS Principle, the 3-4-5 triangle and the two dogs we all own. But most of all they'll know by your words and actions that you love them and have invested your life into them.

So dignify this moment with a special dinner in a private room at a favorite restaurant. The more expensive the better, as you are able. It is important that you gather six or seven key individuals for this. A grandfather/grandmother should fly in if you can possibly arrange it. A coach or perhaps a music instructor may be included. These six people may not all know each other, but make sure they are the few people who have significantly influenced your child's life. Share the planning of the evening together with your child. Dress up, take pictures, and once the meal is done, allow each person around the table to talk to your child directly and personally, concluding with you. In a few minutes each, they should share from their heart and charge your son/daughter to continue in the paths they've been taught, emulating the significant adults sitting around that table. From that night forward, a new relationship will emerge with a young adult who rightly sees a changing role in his or her own life. Be sure you embrace that change and grow with them toward a relationship with a responsible young adult. ***

*** The 18-year-old ceremony is modeled on the writing of Dr. Robert Lewis, Men's Fraternity, Little Rock, Arkansas.

❏ I choose to teach this   Date Completed   _____

_____

_____

Moderation in All Things

John had always had a natural physical ability to run distance. In high school, he lettered in cross-country. As a single adult, he continued this sport and even placed in a regional marathon. Soon he was running over 100 miles per week to train for the more prestigious marathons. He could do this and still balance work, his small group at church and increasing time spent with Susan. He and Susan were married and within a year, their first child was born having special learning disabilities. Suddenly the 100 miles per week was cutting right into infant therapy classes and other commitments. What was a good thing in its proper balance was now taking 20 hours a week away from the essential demands on John and Susan. John realized he was violating the Moderation Principle and cut back to 20 miles per week, even though it meant no more marathons for the foreseeable future.

Sally and Jim found their challenges as a couple going in a little different direction, but the principle was still the same. They found it difficult to say "no" to the worthwhile needs at their small, growing church. They realized that with both of them teaching Sunday School, singing on the worship team, and developing a small group ministry, it was leaving no time for their kids, marriage building or career growth, so they also applied this principle and got back to moderation in all things.

These two examples are clear enough, but let's be aware of one exception to the principle. Moderation in all things can't be used to justify a "moderate" amount of something that is inherently destructive, unbiblical, or otherwise prohibited. A little of a bad thing is still a bad thing.

❏ I choose to teach this   Date Completed   _____

_____

_____

Drinking Alcohol – Going Beyond the Moderation in All Things Principle

In our culture, we must all come to a point of decision on the use of alcohol for ourselves. We have made it illegal for minors because of the inherent risks, but we allow adults to assume personal responsibility to choose whether they will begin drinking. I say begin, because medical research indicates that for some, once that choice is made, the ability to control or stop drinking altogether is much more difficult than for the rest of the population.

So if our children are to make this decision with wisdom and insight rather than by following wherever their peer group leads, it will require us to offer proactive, wise counsel, and example well before the emotional moment of decision. (Lacking any counsel from us, that moment of decision will come years before their 18th birthday.)

Let's consider a few key facts, pro and con, and resolve to first apply it to our own lives and then to discuss it with our pre-teens.

Pro
1. Some foods may taste better with good wine.

2. Some adult peer groups can be uncomfortable if we choose not to drink.

These may not seem very convincing reasons to make a dangerous lifestyle choice, but I don't know of any others.

Con
1. No alcoholic ever planned to end up there. Your ability to control the power of alcohol is unknown before you start drinking. The pain and generational damage done to families by alcoholism cannot be measured. Just ask an ACOA (adult child of alcoholics) man or woman.

2. Driving while even slightly influenced by alcohol can cause an accident that otherwise could have been avoided. A death, serious injury, property damage, pain and suffering, increased insurance

costs and a challenge to our reputation are all risks for the social drinker who drives.

3. Add up the costs of stocking a liquor cabinet and hosting only one party per year for 50 years.

4. While others may say they would rather drink themselves, whom would they want as a neighbor? A surgeon, an airline pilot, etc. – probably someone who they know maintains a personal policy of avoiding alcohol. It becomes a mark of credibility and respect even though their words and actions at close range may do more to justify their own drinking than acknowledging the wisdom of not drinking.

5. Even if you are one of those people who can control your desire for alcohol and even if you have enough money to buy it, and even if you're never in a car accident where alcohol was a factor, can you be sure all that will be true for your kids?

The role model we present will have a great influence on their decision about alcohol, but once the decision is made to include alcohol in their lives, all of these risks repeat themselves through another generation increasing the odds that one or more will eventually occur.

❏ I choose to teach this   Date Completed   _____
                                                          _____
                                                          _____

The Foundations Principle

Several years ago, after Lora Sue and I had moved into our first start-er home, we were energetic about finding ways to improve the property and increase the home's resale value. One of those projects was a small screened in porch off of the master bedroom. I made arrangements for my Uncle Paul to come and help with the job. Actually he had all the skill and I tried to help him. One of the ways I tried to help turned out to be a waste of effort but a lesson that I needed to learn.

About a week before we were to start, I thought I would pour some concrete to serve as a foundation for the 4x4 corner posts. I flattened the ground, even made a little form and then poured out some concrete about 2 inches deep. I even put some coat hangers in to serve as reinforcement. In less than an hour, my job was done. When Paul came, he didn't laugh, he just gave a couple blows with a sledge hammer and it was all in pieces ready for me to carry away. We then proceeded to dig a posthole 40" deep and filled it with concrete. It took several hours to do both holes and it was some of the hardest work of the project.

My efforts are embarrassing to relate now, but how many of us let our kids build part of their lives on "two inches of concrete" when the Foundations Principle would teach us otherwise. The Foundations Principle says: **For every visible, worthwhile, productive result, that stands the test of time; there is a corresponding process of preparation that goes before it.** If it is hurried or avoided, the result may look good at first, but it will soon collapse, leaving a situation worse than if no effort had ever been undertaken.

Just as a foundation is essential for every building project, the principle also holds true for the rest of life.

A foundation is for the most part unseen once the final structure is in place. The work we do preparing for a career or a skill is never visible years later, but the test of time assures you it was there. This is not only true for education. An apprenticeship is another essential element of a successful result. Working with and emulating a master is the pattern for all of life. The comedian, the pastor, or the bricklayer didn't become productive in their field without earning their stripes at the side of a seasoned master. We don't place a bright, energetic graduate as Vice President of Marketing, no matter how charismatic he may be. And in those few cases where it happens, the result is predictably painful.

Unless the Foundations Principle is understood, the risks of shortcuts and costly results are ever-present. We believe we can get something for nothing, maybe just this time. You might sell one or two customers without learning your craft, you might see initial results for a short time in a new employee, but unless the unseen foundation is there, expect the structure to come down.

Peter said to the leaders of the early church, "Young men, in the same way, be submissive to those who are older. Clothe yourselves with humility toward one another for God opposes the proud but gives grace to the humble. Humble yourselves therefore under the mighty hand of God that he may lift you up in due time."

This principle was just more theory until the wet, spring day in May of 1997 when I took my boys to the construction site of the new Target store near our house. We walked through some mud but I couldn't resist the opportunity for a memorable lesson. Only the walls were up and some of the foundation pads were poured. Huge 8' x 8' holes were being filled with concrete. These foundations would later hold up the poles or I-beams in the center of the store that would support the roof. Today, that store is done. You can't see the foundations but my boys know they are there. Visit a construction site. Then talk about how important the unseen foundation is for buildings and for people.

❏ I choose to teach this   Date Completed   _____

_____

_____

Quit While They're Still Applauding

Our kids may never sing or dance before a packed house, but sooner or later, we all perform in some way before an audience. It may be a brief presentation at work or it might be a discussion at a neighborhood meeting where we try to persuade friends and strangers at the same time. Or, it may actually be a musical solo. They all have this in common: Your audience will judge your presentation – they will agree or disagree – based on their feelings when you are <u>finished</u>. Let me say that in a different way. If you are succeeding in your presentation, the song is going great, the group is interested in your talk, or the class seems to be connecting with your every word; the natural tendency is to keep doing what you're doing. But the exact opposite should be your goal, that is, to realize sooner than later, your appeal will dull and their overall response will be based on your final moments.

In business this is called "stop selling once you have the order." It could also be called "stop talking once you've made your point." We all appreciate, respect and probably want to support the man who makes a valid point even though it may be in opposition to our original thinking. If that same man, however, just keeps pounding on the issue, we're likely to have time and the desire to construct all kinds of opposing reasons in our own mind. At that point, the day is lost for the presenter and continuing to talk will only make matters worse.

Discuss this principle with your pre-teens, explaining how too much of a good thing is a bad thing and how people develop their opinion of the presentation. It may be a concert that ran too long or a sermon that was thought provoking for the first 30 minutes, but when your kids have just experienced this for themselves, then discuss how their response would have been better if the presenter had only quit while they were still applauding.

❑ I choose to teach this   Date Completed   _____

_____

_____

Self Esteem in Spite of Personal Liabilities

Whether we would easily admit it or not, we view our kids' success in school, and relationships in life as a direct reflection on us as parents. And to a large extent, this is true, considering their genetic make-up and intellectual aptitude is directly downloaded from mom and dad.

But that's only one part of the mixture, the recipe, that will one day leave your house pretty much in its final form.

What are those other factors, those other elements of the recipe that affect every son or daughter? And let's remember that these factors are equally true for the bright talented child who finds it easy to coast through school with good grades as they are for the less gifted child who struggles with self-esteem.

Here are two factors that I think hold water.

1. A child who has some obvious weaknesses but also has the strong, positive affirmation from his father will often experience more personal and professional success than the gifted child whom everyone thought didn't need much encouragement.

   When was the last time you picked up your young boy and with a thrill in your voice said "You're terrific-you're my favorite 6 year old in the whole world?" Modest achievement with the <u>involvement</u> and approval of their dad does more to build the man or woman than the blue ribbon that dad never noticed. And not just in sports. Sports have merit, but participation and success in the things that have a closer correlation to adult challenges will build even more into your child's confidence and self esteem. The speech tournament, the school play, the science fair, selling cookies door to door to raise funds for a worthy cause—all these and many more are opportunities for you to create a success experience with your child.

2. The other factor is one that I believe relates especially to the child with intellectual or other personal liabilities. How many times have you as an experienced adult observed someone with less talent or aptitude than you who has really made it? Of course, we all have. And how many bright "most likely to succeed" types are still

job-hopping with limited success as they approach 50? If we think about it, it's clear that finding your niche is perhaps even more critical to our personal and professional success as adults than the innate talent or intellect. You don't read well enough to be an editor? You have an attention deficit that makes it hard to concentrate for extended periods? These are very real problems that require specific attention, but I personally know men (and you probably do too) who have found career paths that don't rely on their weaknesses, but rely on their areas of strength. Find one of these men or women who share your child's liability but who have clearly achieved success and fulfillment in their niche in life. Get to know them and set up a time where they can tell their story in a private one-on-one with your son or daughter.

As you work with and affirm your son or daughter, explain that you're not just giving them positive fluff, but that together, you can acknowledge their weaknesses and know that there are career paths that will allow them to achieve remarkable success and satisfaction with the tools that God has given them.

❑ I choose to teach this   Date Completed   _____

_____

_____

Don't Get Upset Over the Things You Can't Control

In an earlier chapter, I shared my experience in the summer of 1975, selling books door-to-door for the Southwestern Company of Nashville, TN. Those 17 weeks were a boot camp for many of life's lessons. One lesson they drummed into us from the first day was "Don't get upset over the things you can't control." When you're 19 and you've worked smart and hard through a hot, humid summer, delivered your product on time, but that nice personable housewife writes you a bad check, most of us would get upset. Time was limited, however, and with hundreds of other customers to deliver, there was no way to travel back many miles to try to collect. It was a situation that, after the fact, could not be controlled.

I <u>could</u> have gotten upset. That might have had several interesting results. Let's consider a few.

1. I could have delivered a torrent of strong language to her absent ears. Now I'd be even more upset, ready to insult my next customer who was honest and prepared to pay on time, while the target of my anger never heard a word.

2. I could have expended my anger on the accelerator of my car. That might have resulted in a $75 ticket.

3. I could have given up and never approached the next 10 customers who were honest and eager to buy books from a college boy. At $30 each, that's…well, you get the idea.

The only profitable response is to learn whatever you can and choose not to get upset over the things you can't control. In my case, I might have learned never to take a check for a final payment. Usually the learning opportunity isn't so obvious, however. It's usually a simple matter that we take calculated, reasonable actions and the results still go south. If we had it to do over again, we'd do the same thing.

For your teens, it may be that after hard work on the sports field, the coach still doesn't play them. Or, on an important first date, traffic backs up, making them late for the date <u>and</u> meeting the parents.

I never realized back in 1975 how firmly rooted this principle was in Scripture. When Paul, the great apologist for the Christian faith, was in an awful, dirty Roman prison, he refused to get upset over the things he couldn't control. Writing to the Philippians he said, "For I have learned to be content whatever the circumstances. I know what it is to be in need, and I know what it is to have plenty...I can do everything through him who gives me strength."

It's not that we deny the pain and loss of the situation, but we can choose how we react since getting upset will not do any good and likely will create all kinds of new harm. Think about it! It's bad enough what just happened to you. So why get upset and take foolish actions that will cause new problems and add to your emotional pain?

Share this principle with your kids and invite them to call you on it when something truly out of your control tempts you to get upset.

❑ I choose to teach this   Date Completed   _____

_____

_____

Action Precedes Emotion

Do you remember Cliff Claven from the Cheers TV bar? He was an expert about everything – especially the U.S. postal service. Never mind that his friends at the bar could care less about his adventures on the mail delivery route.

How interested are you in gardening? Not very? Well, how about planning a special date with your wife that includes hidden clues to help her guess what you've planned for the evening? If you're like most of us, both sound like a lot of work. Not something that has much positive emotion for us.

Think now for a minute about the things you <u>would</u> like to spend your time doing. A tennis match or a round of golf. Building a shelf at your own pace, or writing a blog on the internet. All of them have one thing in common; you have done it before, probably several times, and have become something of an expert. We are never interested in something that is new and foreign, especially if it sounds like work. But you've heard it before that "it's only work if you're not having fun." The more we take action to learn about something, investing our time, becoming more knowledgeable and skilled, the more we will enjoy the event – we'll experience at least a few positive <u>emotions</u>.

So the principle works like this: When faced with a task or responsibility that seems to be dull, lifeless or even repulsive, most of us put it off. We find excuses to delay the inevitable. If we delay too long, circumstances become even more negative than they were originally. Instead, we would do well to remember the times in our own experience when we didn't really want to get involved at first, but the more we got into it, the more our interest and motivation grew.

I grant you, there are some things that you and I may never find very interesting no matter how hard we try. But if Cliff Claven is interested in the postal service, and if your friends are interested in the things they know so well, we can learn the principle and demonstrate it to our kids that action precedes emotion. Get into it, learn about it, try it a time or two and we'll be surprised at what we may find interesting.

❑ I choose to teach this   Date Completed   _____

_____

_____

Personal Presence

What is it about some people who seem to have a more commanding personal presence than most others? They aren't arrogant or proud – that would be easily spotted. No, they just seem to have a strong, and often quiet, personal confidence. It is a quality that produces trust and respect from those around them.

This kind of intangible character quality is the result of many factors that go beyond our discussion here, but there are six simple actions that will greatly improve our own confidence and give our kids a big jump start compared to other teens or young adults.

1. **Eye Contact:** The ability to look steadily and deeply into someone's eyes during a conversation speaks louder than your words. It says you have nothing to hide. Most adults cannot bear this feeling of exposure, so they glance away quickly in their own conversations. Even if the listener isn't consciously aware of this dynamic, they unconsciously feel superior because of the other's lack of personal confidence and so they feel comfortable acting superior. Now, you can't burn a hole in your counterpart. That raises their sensibilities in the other direction, it feels overbearing and pushy. No, the idea is to present a quiet confidence and your eyes are an essential part of that. Remember the 4-second rule. Look steadily into someone's eyes while counting slowly to four. It will seem like an eternity at first but do it anyway.

2. **Handshake:** Most adults are aware of this, so some overdo it and try to take your arm off. For teens and young adults, however, offering a handshake to a man or responding to the hand of a woman is a positive part of your personal presence. Not so strong or weak as to be noticeable, just doing it without hesitation.

3. **Walking Speed:** Have a little fun with your kids when you're waiting in the car or in a shopping mall. Play the walking game. Observe someone walking by and then make up stories about what they do, what they're thinking and where they are going. The game automatically teaches this principle: A brisk walk says this

person is going somewhere and knows where he is going. Posture and body language cannot be avoided while walking. For better or worse, they advertise how you feel about yourself. The principle that "Action Precedes Emotion" even applies here. Walk with a spring in your step, pick up the pace just slightly and two things happen—you will begin to feel better about yourself and others will subconsciously notice your self confidence and assume it is justified.

4. **Speak Up:** It is hard to hear someone who timidly offers their words, but even worse, it advertises their lack of personal confidence. If you don't believe in your words enough to speak up, how can you expect your listeners to believe them? I'm reminded of the proverb that says "Even a fool is thought to be wise until he opens his mouth." Better to say nothing than to advertise the fact that I don't have the confidence to speak loud enough for everyone to comfortably hear me. As this relates to our kids, it is normal that teens or young adults will feel intimidated in a group of older adults. This does not need to be the case. Knowing their place and avoiding arrogance and impropriety is another subject, but when it is proper for young people to speak, then speak up. For us as dads, in addition to discussing this subject directly, we are the most important factor in building their self-confidence in this area as we listen and validate their thoughtful opinions at home.

5. **Sit in the Front:** Most of us naturally choose to sit near the back in a classroom or seminar. We feel less conspicuous. We can blend into the crowd near the back. That's true. If you want to blend into the crowd, sit near the back, but if you want to get more out of the teacher's presentation and subtly set yourself apart from the crowd, choose a seat near the front. If you were the teacher, how would you feel and what assumptions would you make about the person who chose to sit near the front?

6. **Smile:** Of all these actions that contribute to our self-confidence and personal presence, smiling may be the most beneficial. A smile says: "I like you, I like this situation, I'm comfortable in this situation, I like me." A smile, when it is genuine and sincere, puts the other person at ease while at the same time improving your own feelings about the moment. A smile speaks of confidence while a blank stare or wrinkled brow is a sure sign of fear

and uneasiness. A smile is an action that precedes the emotion of quiet confidence.

None of these actions will come automatically to a young man or woman, but have fun with it. Touch on the subject often so that when it's time for the college interview or first job, these actions will already be proven in your children's experience.

Credit: Most of these ideas were originally put forward by D. J. Schwartz, The Magic of Thinking Big, Cornerstone, 1959.

❑ I choose to teach this   Date Completed   _____

_____

_____

Work Smart, Not Just Hard

Oh, don't get me wrong. Very little of real value is accomplished without hard work. But too often, we go right to the hard work and don't stop long enough to think, to plan, what it is that will yield the greatest results.

Several years ago, our company instituted a Quality Advantage program. To help the theory take root in our everyday actions, several phrases became part of the company vocabulary. One of those phrases was "doing right things, right." That is to say, working smart (taking the time to figure out what is the right thing to do) and working hard (doing that right thing, RIGHT).

A two dimensional matrix helps to visualize what can happen when we do, or don't take time to work smart before we work hard.

WORK

	Easy	Hard
THINKING — Thoughtless	1	2
THINKING — Smart	3	4

1. This quadrant is where fools live. They not only choose to take it easy, they aren't really sure what they're trying to do. But its not only fools in this corner. Well-intentioned people who are just too busy to consider this issue at all can find themselves living here.

2. Hard workers who mean well will accomplish some good and valuable results. Even if they fall into it by accident, their dedication and sincerity will yield some results. Expect to see some progress at work and children reared in consistent, solid homes. We have to give some credit here because, let's face it, most of the world lives here. Still, it's a shame how much effort is wasted.

3. Working smart but with little effort is probably represented by the smallest group. It is rare that a person has the wisdom and foresight to evaluate a short term or long term challenge and still fails to put in any serious effort on the things that matter to them. You and I have seen them though. You can tell they're insightful, and from time to time they accomplish something with seeming ease, but for the most part they're content to produce mediocre results in whatever arena they're involved.

4. Working at the right things, and working hard is the only combination that will consistently yield lasting, positive results.

The woodcutter needs to be smart enough to sharpen his axe and then willing to swing hard. The combination of those two will fell a lot of trees.

Draw the matrix and discuss this concept with your pre-teen. Then be prepared when he asks you next Saturday if you're working smart or just hard.

❑ I choose to teach this   Date Completed   _____

_____

_____

Small Acts of Unexpected Generosity Reap Great Rewards

Many people are generous, at times. They may give their money and even their valuable time. If it comes from a cheerful heart and a humble spirit, it is a joyful thing to see, especially if you are fortunate enough to be on the receiving end. If our generosity is the result of an appeal to help meet a specific need, our response may be partly expected. Sometimes it can even swing to the other extreme—don't respond and you're viewed as a mean spirited Scrooge. The key to making the greatest impact is when generosity comes unexpectedly to meet a genuine need and it comes from a humble and cheerful giver.

It doesn't always have to be costly to the giver—just valued by the receiver. Remembering a person's name and addressing them with it is a small but valued act of generosity.

Several years ago, Larry, a friend of mine had agreed to raise funds for a project he supported. He got ten friends to give $50 each. Since he served as the organization's local treasurer, he accepted the ten $50 gifts, but before he could pass them along to headquarters, he lost the envelope of checks. It was an honest mistake. I knew it and he knew it, but the appearance of impropriety or at the least, sloppy handling made him reluctant and embarrassed to go back to the donors. You can imagine our surprise when he told me how one of the ten original donors responded by saying "Larry, you're probably not going to get all ten to write you another check, so let me replace mine with $100 so you're not left holding the bag."

Not a big thing? Maybe not, but I saw the strong impression it made on Larry. Why? Because it was unexpected. It's not only how much is given, it is the gift (money, time, effort, etc.) relative to what the recipient expects. That same $50 gift would have gone unnoticed in circumstances where large gifts were the norm, but for Larry, the circumstances made the gift one he'll never forget.

Let us understand this part of human nature and explain it at a time when we can discuss motives and standards with our teens.

❏ I choose to teach this   Date Completed   _____
                                                      _____
                                                      _____

Character in an Age of Superstars

Definition of Character: **"The sum of all the accumulated private decisions and actions that make us what we really are."**

In an age when our culture's heroes are millionaire sports figures, rap performers, celebutantes and overnight movie stars, we don't need to spend much time here establishing the fact that, with few exceptions, these media creations are not positive character role models for our kids.

We've always had cultural heroes, but the modern media apparatus creates an inverse relationship that gives enormous wealth and associated power to younger people than would otherwise have developed that level of earning power. Wealth and power corrupt, so it is no wonder that a $6 million per year 24 year old is likely to act and speak in ways that are an awful role model for kids who, like the superstar, are still developing their own character.

What are the virtues that most assuredly identify someone who has accumulated those difficult private decisions and actions? Here are just a few:

Patience: When our lives don't match up to someone else's overnight success.

Gratitude: For our family.
              For our country's freedom and past generations
              that give a watershed of economic potential.
              For God and salvation through faith in Jesus Christ.

Honesty: Especially when it takes courage to come clean.

Integrity: Knowing that my private moments match my public image.

Humility: Having the confidence to allow someone else to appear superior.

Reliability: Making good on your word regardless of personal effort and cost.

Work: Knowing that God created it good from the beginning.

Courage: Acting against the tide of the moment.

Faith: Drawing personal strength from knowing that our lives and our eternal spirits are in the hands of a loving God.

Remember the difference between virtues and values. Use these non-negotiable virtues as a standard to measure some of the culture's heroes. With your pre-teens, see how many of these virtues expose a superstar's true character—for better or worse.

Let me share one example of a conversation that created a lasting memory in our house. When our son Colson was 10, we were having some McDonalds together one day, when I asked him if he could tell me what integrity was. He made a good attempt, but I explained that it actually means consistency – flawless throughout – no fake or missing parts. Then I said, "Imagine a brick wall with no cement, just 100 bricks perfectly stacked into a wall." He was definitely with me. I said, "What would happen if you pulled one of the bricks out of the center? Would it be 99% as good as the perfect wall?" "No," he agreed. "It would be almost worthless and it might fall apart." In the literal definition, that wall no longer has integrity. "That's the way it is with you and me," I said. "If we have secret sins but act like we are consistent throughout, we lose strength and confidence just like that brick wall – we don't have integrity."

❏ I choose to teach this   Date Completed   _____

_____

_____

First Impressions

Think, for a moment, about your first introduction to your wife, or your best, trusted friend. Was it a 10? Maybe not. But over time, circumstances brought you together in a way that led to trust, respect and love.

Most of our relationships, however, are not like this. How could they be? There isn't time or energy to build very many deep and trusted relationships. Our relationships look something like a pyramid. Steeper for some of us, wider for others, but necessarily a pyramid. Draw this illustration on a napkin and have the discussion with your teen.

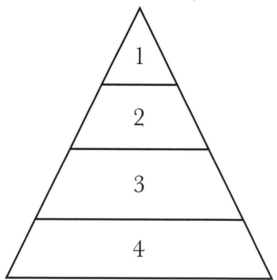

1. Our wife and one or two intimate friends. They know our weaknesses and love us anyway. Maybe three people.

2. Work, church, neighborhood friends we enjoy, see socially, and know pretty well. Maybe 15-20 people.

3. Supervisors or subordinates we must interact with less often. We don't know each other well. We each rely heavily on first impressions and see ongoing actions in the context of what we already believe about each other. Maybe 100-150 people.

4. Acquaintances who have their own opinions, based almost entirely on first impressions or distant observation. Very little opportunity to change their impressions. Maybe 1,000 people.

Have you ever received a strong, positive referral? Your first meeting takes on a completely different flavor than if you introduced yourself cold. Same person, but the strong first impression carries the relationship forward quickly.

For level 1 relationships and a few in level 2, time and repeated exposure will overshadow a weak first impression. The depth of your character and abilities will come out no matter how the first meeting went. The problem is, levels 1 and 2 only account for a few percent of the people who know us and affect our lives. We'll never have the time to reveal our true personal strengths to the other 95%. In most cases, our first impression, good or bad, will never be reversed.

Our early teens will understand that only a few people will ever see our personal strengths from repeated interaction. Use positive and negative examples of people you both know from each of the four levels to explain how important first impressions are.

❏ I choose to teach this   Date Completed   _____

_____

_____

Firecrackers and Rifle Shots
(The Strategic and Disciplined Use of Power)

When I was 8 or 9, I thought it was exciting to take one or two firecrackers, tear them apart carefully, and spill the gunpowder into a small pile on the garage floor. By touching a match to it, a momentary and bright flare would burn. Only a puff of smoke would remain after the short burst of the flare. My dad was a hunter and I can also remember going elk hunting together. Dad's rifle was a 30-0-6. It fired a bullet using about as much powder as my flare in the garage, but as we both know, the results were very different. The bullet could bring down a 900 pound elk, while the firecracker had no real purpose except to attract momentary attention.

You and I have been placed into positions of power and influence. Maybe it's not much on the surface, but how and when we choose to express ourselves can bring results as different as a firecracker or a big game bullet.

The wise man will carefully fire his bullet knowing exactly what he needs to accomplish, aiming carefully so that people or other valuables are not damaged. The fool, on the other hand, will throw his firecracker while his emotions are still high. The result is little or no permanent change, just a loud, annoying sound for a moment, followed by a stinking cloud that tends to remain.

So how can we avoid throwing firecrackers? Never respond to a situation while your emotions are hot. Wait hours or days if necessary until you can think through what the mature, Christ-like and respected response would be, knowing that every firecracker response builds a reputation of a fairly harmless but annoying adolescent who never accomplishes something of lasting consequence. Then after thinking, praying and considering your objective, act or speak so that a small amount of "gun powder" will bring the greatest result.

❏ I choose to teach this   Date Completed   _____

_____

_____

Meeting and Working with Powerful People

You've experienced it – so have I – and as much as we try to be ourselves, meeting and working with powerful people makes most of us act uncomfortable. Usually their power is somehow tied to money, so we should expand this point to include wealthy and/or powerful people. It may be a potential employer with the power to hire you. It may be a relative or a neighbor. We're not close enough to have overcome the inferiority that we feel, so we try to disguise our feelings with formal talk or other actions that only shine a spotlight on our differences.

Lets be reminded of three things when we're tempted to "fake it" around rich or powerful people.

1. They can see it a mile away.

2. It doesn't help your cause at all.

3. It sets you both up. They feel superior and you feel inferior.

If you want to further your cause and feel surprisingly good about this brief encounter, concentrate on five things:

1. Smile

2. Make eye contact with them.

3. Say what you mean – plainly.

4. Show real respect for their time schedule.

5. Listen – really listen.

A smile says I'm the warm, honest, real person you see and your eyes are the front door that confidently invites them into your life. Be sure of what it is that <u>you</u> have that could benefit <u>them</u>.

If you can accomplish this, you'll be a rare commodity in the experience of most rich and powerful people. Wait until your son or daughter has watched or experienced first hand the awkward moment of meeting someone whom they perceive as having power over their life. Then have this discussion together.

❑ I choose to teach this   Date Completed   _____

_____

_____

Earned Responsibility, Mutual Expectations and Consequences

As adults, we live and work in a world that, with some exceptions, delivers consequences based on our actions. If we skip work, we'll have to answer for it. If we do it again, we'll likely be looking for a new job. If we really like that 22-foot boat and buy it on a credit card, Visa has only one simple response: pay the interest or life will get very unpleasant – no exceptions. For our kids this process of growing from childhood discipline to adolescent responsibility is as basic as a bird learning to flap its wings and fly.

Remember the cone in chapter 1? This transition must gradually take place so that our teenagers' actions are the result of their having tested and tasted real world consequences. At the beginning, we will set the bar low. But once it's set, we must allow them to knock it down through irresponsibility and feel the minor consequences. If we continue to threaten to apply manual or artificial consequences (punishment) they will grow up believing that life's circumstances are a matter of how hard they beg (or demand), and the benevolence of the authority figure.

Nothing is more tragic and pitiful than a young adult who still acts as though adult consequences can be gained or avoided by childish manipulation. Proverbs says it like this: "Provocation by a fool is heavier than sand and rocks."

It is up to us as dads to strategically plan where and when we set the bar and then allow our kids to experience the age appropriate consequences when they knock it down.

Dignify this process. Make it a familiar ritual to sit down and together with your child, agree on the expectation and consequences for failure and success. Does your 16-year-old want to drive the family car? I believe they should pay the insurance increase on your policy and their own gas. What if they get a ticket? Factor in consequences before they happen so there is a shared agreement. By the time they leave home at about 18 and the cone has come to a point, our opportunity to guide this crucial part of their growth is basically over. They're going to experience earned consequences. The question is whether they will come in loving, measured doses now or from the blunt edge of life later.

Note: Manually protecting them from life's consequences after they have left home only delays the inevitable, making it more traumatic when reality eventually hits. It also points to our own failure as dads to deal with this back when we should have.

❏ I choose to teach this   Date Completed   _____

_____

_____

You Get Out What You Put In

There are many ways to say it – "It takes money to make money" or "You can't reap what you don't sow." The Bible says, "Whatever a man sows, that will he also reap." The verse is usually applied to mean that if we spend our time and talents positively, we'll see a worthwhile result.

But I think there is another perspective on this principle that says if you give a small effort, (even at a good thing) you'll reap a small result, and vice versa. Is your son discouraged, lethargic and procrastinating on his science project? Putting in a minimal effort is sure to result in a modest result with little or no personal satisfaction and he still had to work his way out of neutral. In short, it wasn't worth it. If, however, he can choose to make a stronger effort, it will almost certainly produce a solid project as well as the pride and sense of accomplishment that goes with it. Result: It was worth it.

Only the years and a positive example of this principle will ever produce a young adult who can both know this principle in their head and apply it with their feet.

Most adults live their life largely controlled by their circumstances, rarely if ever understanding this principle. But the young adult who at least understands this principle and has experienced its truth even a few times, stands a real chance to live much of their life in control of their own circumstances.

❏ I choose to teach this   Date Completed   _____

_____

_____

The Rich Heritage in our American History

Unless you're part of the 3% of the population that enjoyed high school history and attended a private school, you may need a little convincing on this one. Part of the reason for this is that late 20th century public education and discourse has stripped away any reference to God and the Biblical faith of our founding fathers, leaving only sterile, one dimensional figures in our history books. When we read about George Washington, it is more likely to include the cherry tree story than the text of his inaugural address or a recounting of his prayers during the Valley Forge winter. Thanks to Disney, Pocahontas is known as a nature loving Indian girl, but no mention is made that her conversion to faith in Jesus Christ and baptism is commemorated with a mural in the United States Capitol Rotunda.

Regardless of whether the historical event includes evidence of Godly faith, whenever we can visit the actual sights and learn the lesser-known pieces of the historical puzzle, it is only natural that our kids, and we, will find history coming to life. This principle is true for any historical inquiry, but for those of us who want to show our kids that the God of the Bible is the God of history, the early American record abounds with interesting and even shocking examples of God's involvement in the lives and events of our founding fathers. Truly, God did shed his grace on us.

Peter Marshall and David Manual have written two books that trace God's hand of blessing and intervention in America's history. The Light and the Glory begins with Columbus and ends with Washington. From Sea to Shining Sea moves from the War of Independence to the spreading of the nation across the continent.

Use these references or many others to get a foothold, but make at least one trip to the East Coast that brings your family face to face with the rich, Godly heritage in the people and events of our American history. If you don't, don't expect them to get it in public schools.

❑ I choose to teach this   Date Completed   _____

_____

_____

God Isn't Predictable and Life Isn't Fair

It is interesting that the very concept of fairness, right vs. wrong, is evidence for the existence of God. If there were no God, how then could man have any innate, mutually agreed sense of justice or fairness? But more problematic for those of us who already believe there is a God, is our sense that life isn't fair and that all too often we're on the short end of the scale.

The Bible says that, "...as high as the heavens are above the earth, so high are his thoughts above ours...". Why does a child die before he has a chance to experience any of life's joys? Why does a young mother die when her children and husband need and love her? Why is one student naturally smart while your child struggles and still achieves only limited progress? King David and Job were both Godly men who struggled with the apparent success of others – especially the unbelievers around them. But like them, we must put it to rest in our own minds and model this acceptance for our kids. "The Lord gives and the Lord takes away – blessed be the name of the Lord." We must resolve not to waste a lot of time wondering why – wishing things were different, but accept the building blocks God has given us and honor Him by building as much as those blocks will allow. We all know the stories of the great achievements by Beethoven, Fanny Crosby, Roosevelt and countless others who refused to believe that their disabilities made it impossible for them to succeed. Their progress brought additional honor to the God who gave them their original position in life.

The flip side of this is also true. Those who have been blessed with health, wealth, brains or talent, should not feel guilty and expect that God will surely take it away before long since this just isn't fair. No, that's the whole point of the principle. He's the one who gave the talent in the first place. He only promises to love and groom us the way we love our sons or daughters, regardless of their skills or talents. But then unlike us, in His infinite wisdom and love, He reserves the right to exercise the role of God in our lives.

❏ I choose to teach this   Date Completed   _____

_____

_____

One's Reputation – Its Value, Source and Durability

Our reputation is a priceless personal asset. It is unstoppable. It grows and develops whether we like it or not. It is built from the time tested truth of what we really are, not what we would like to be. In one sense it is out of our control since a reputation is what others believe to be true about us. They may see only a part of our total being or learn the truth that we thought was a well-kept secret.

In a greater sense, however, it is entirely within our control. We, alone, can choose the private and public actions, which accumulate like small pieces in a mosaic. The true picture emerges, and once painted, it can never be washed away – only added to.

A reputation can be so strong that it affects the entire family or organization that we are part of, for better or for worse.

Be on the look out for teachable moments when yours or someone else's reputation becomes the decisive factor in events that are understandable and important to your kids.

❏ I choose to teach this   Date Completed   _____

_____

_____

The Principle of Delegation and its Leveraged Effectiveness

"If you want a job done right, do it yourself," right? That old adage has some truth to it. In fact, the Hired Hand Principle (p. 72) seems to support it. But it only applies for a single task in one place at one time. Ongoing projects intended to touch many people over time will require delegation.

The principle of delegation and its leveraged effectiveness was once described to me as the difference between $1+2+3+4+5$ and $1\times2\times3\times4\times5$. Delegation is more difficult. It takes more patience. In fact, like the example, at first you may see less result than if you focused and did the job yourself. But allow a little time to pass and the man who invests himself in others, teaching, showing, encouraging, and rewarding them – he will accomplish things that could never be done by one man if his whole life were spent on the project.

The obvious example of this is the Lord Jesus. He had infinite powers, yet He chose to delegate the building of the first century Church to twelve men.

It is important to recognize also, that the skills needed to effectively delegate and produce results through others are not at all similar to the skills of the talented but independent individual. To delegate requires us to work patiently with the only building blocks God made – people. Some of these blocks are odd shaped. They don't lay flat and fit together easily. This points to yet another skill required of the one who delegates – being able to pick the right block for the right place in the wall. Within the church, Scripture says we are to use our talents and spiritual gifts/abilities according as God has enabled us. Recognizing those natural inclinations and abilities is the job of the one who delegates.

The talented but independent loner, who has not developed the patience or skills to work through others will be limited to achieving only what he can create by himself. But the son or daughter who learns early on the difference between $1+2+3+4+5$ and $1\times2\times3\times4\times5$ will be on his way to accomplishing great things through delegation.

❏ I choose to teach this   Date Completed   _____

_____

_____

111

Jobs Expand to Fill the Time Available

If you think about it, we've all observed this principle at work in our own lives. You know the report isn't due for three weeks and even though you planned to finish it before leaving for vacation – well, you know. It works in reverse, too. I oversleep until there's only 35 minutes until the train leaves. It's funny how the same functions that normally take 45 minutes in the morning can be done in 25 when you have to.

These are simple examples, but the principle is true for large and small issues alike. We don't plan it that way, but unless we guard that precious commodity of time, we tend to finish just on time or acceptably late. How much could have been done to improve or increase our results if we had only maintained control instead of riding along as we watch the project perfectly fill all the time allowed.

It's easy to see this fact played out in the lives of others so I suggest, on this one, use others or a personal example when you discuss this with your pre-teen. Don't point out the 22 times in the past week when it has been true in their life. Seeing it in others and your life will keep their defenses down and allow them to see it in the mirror on their own.

❑ I choose to teach this   Date Completed   _____

_____

_____

Offer Your Kids 10 Questions to Discuss When Considering Marriage, Beyond the Obvious Issues of Love and Spiritual Unity

The day will come when your kids will begin thinking they have met their God given mate. They may have, but add this quiz to your other counsel[****].

1. Have I seen my potential mother and father in law in REAL LIFE? I should expect my spouse will bear a remarkable similarity.

2. Are their family vacation habits similar to my own vacation experiences?

3. Are their family's gift giving habits and expectations similar to mine?

4. Is my dad's role and our expectations of him similar to the role their father has?

5. Is my mother's role and our expectations of her similar to the role their mother has?

6. Can you confidently say you and your sweetheart have discussed child discipline, and how you feel about how you were disciplined as children?

7. How much money was there in their family and how relatively loose or frugal was it used? Who ran the family finances?

[****] Not that we should require "yes" answers to all these questions, but family patterns in one generation will be issues in the next, and discussing them with a potential mate will be an excellent learning experience, often deepening the relationship in the process.

8. If your sweetheart continued to demonstrate the same personal/character qualities for the next 50 years that you can observe from the past 5 or 10, how would you like it? (They will)

9. What are the most painful memories from each of your childhoods? Share them openly.

10. What are the happiest memories from each of your childhoods? Share them openly.

You might want to add 2 or 3 more based on your own experience.

1.

2.

3.

If these questions raise problems, or more likely, if you don't have solid answers to each one, take however long you need to find out. Believe me, years from now, a few months will not be an issue, and the process of working through these questions together may greatly strengthen or weaken your resolve. And isn't that what you're looking for?

❏ I choose to teach this   Date Completed   _____

_____

_____

The Personal Mission Statement

Think, for a moment, about all the hats you and I wear. As dads we are called upon to be a husband, father, worker/provider, and basic to all of these, a man. For most of us the list doesn't stop there. If you're like me, there are other areas of your life that require you to consistently work with other people, where you have a stake in the success or failure of that organization. Maybe you're a coach or perhaps you are in leadership of a civic organization or your church. Whatever the hat, you care deeply about it or you wouldn't be investing your time and heart there.

But how do we get a grip on all of these different roles at once? My wife needs me to be a listener and a leader at the same time, but my work and church need me to be something very different if I hope to be effective.

Some guys are so close to the trees, they don't even know how big their forest is. They try feverishly just to react to life's demands, but are still frustrated because they're uncertain of what it is, in the final analysis, they are really trying to do in each of their roles. We've all felt this. We try hard to be effective, but the target is so ambiguous we don't know if we're hitting it.

I believe that's it. The target is too broad and ambiguous. Right there is the key to gaining a sense of focus and peace about what we're supposed to do and be. A personal mission statement breaks down our many roles into manageable parts. Whatever the name, it was a freeing and fulfilling exercise for me to simply identify the different roles in my life (that was the easy part) and then make a brief statement about what I really wanted to do and be <u>in that area</u>. A statement that would serve as a measuring stick, a standard against which I could judge my actions in that area. "Does this project pass when seen in the light of my 'work' mission statement?", or, " In the past three months, have my interactions with my kids squared up to my 'father' mission statement?"

If this still sounds a little murky, let me share with you my personal mission statement. Yours may be very different, but I think it will help to see how each role has different objectives.

Graydon J. Hauser
Personal Mission Statement
Proactively address the circumstances in my life – not react – and in so doing, create more of my life's circumstances.
To live by faith and integrity towards true principles and God's promises.

Individual: View every day and week in light of my physical, mental, social and spiritual self. To keep the 7 habits top of mind. To think BIG, not average.
To be a strong finisher.

Husband: To support / facilitate Lora Sue to be the best she can be. To strive for a marriage centered home.

Father: To work hard at learning, communicating and living life's great truths to my boys. To gradually transfer responsibility toward age 18.

Church: To lead the local church toward more authentic discipleship and being salt and light in the world.

Work: To work smart, offering the ATS principle to internal and external customers.

Trying to get a grip or a clear picture of your whole life at once is a sure way to fail at this. So start by listing the five or six areas where you are a key player. Then give one or two brief goals that will help you judge yourself and evaluate your actions in this role. You'll be surprised how much peace and satisfaction comes when you know your actions square up to your own mission statement. (Hint: this is not a one-draft project.)

Once you've given this some thought yourself, do it with your teenagers. They have life roles too and they will benefit from your setting the direction here. Even the process itself will be positive for your teens as they see that you validate the roles they currently have, even though they are different from yours.

Many of these ideas were originated by Stephen R. Covey and discussed in depth in "The Seven Habits of Highly Effective People" Simon & Schuster, 1991

❑ I choose to teach this   Date Completed   _____

_____

_____

Spend Twice as Much on Half as Much

It's only normal to try to find the best bargain when we look for clothes. Some of us hate the process of shopping so much that we pass the whole effort to our wives. (For many of us we would do well to follow more of their advice in this area.) In most families, finances are limited, so the temptation is to pay less for our clothes. But unlike cars or other items where prices are heavily influenced by brand name status, the price of men's clothes is much more a reflection of their real workmanship and overall quality. A quality suit will last much longer than a cheap one, and even when it begins to show signs of wear, its quality is still evident. In the long run, you may actually spend less with the "twice as much for half as much" principle and all the while, people will surprise you by assuming that the man in the suit is of the same quality as his clothes. (Obviously, this also goes for other furnishings – especially shoes.)

You can only wear one change of clothes at a time. There is very little merit in owning 10 suits if they all advertise you as less than you are. Much better to own only 3 suits that convince people of your credibility even before you've said a word.

This may all come across as shallow to some. But it's a fact of life so we can use it to our advantage or allow our appearance to fight against the skill, training and character that we may truly possess.

When our sons go to their first serious job interview, most of us are conscientious that they are dressed for it. In this case the value of their appearance is actually less since the employer is fully aware of their beginner status. But in our everyday lives where we all make subconscious evaluations of others many times a day, the impact of our appearance is more than we might think. So don't worry if you can only afford a little. Make sure you spend twice as much on half as much.

This principle can be learned and appreciated by an 18-year-old, but really only applies when they leave the college campus and begin navigating in the adult arena.

(This principle was originated by Dr. David Schwartz—The Magic of Thinking Big, Cornerstone Library, 1959.)

❏ I choose to teach this   Date Completed   _____
                                                      _____
                                                      _____

The Salary and Position
or Who You Work For

"The decision to buy a cheap suit only feels good when you pay for it." This homespun advice actually applies to a lot more than quality retail purchases. In the area of our employment, many of us have learned that one job may pay a little more to start, the title may sound a little better, but if the company behind the paycheck and title isn't quality, you've bought a cheap suit. And, like a bad suit of clothes, it doesn't take long before the market weaknesses, the management systems that don't quite fit together and some poor quality individual components combine into a situation that will not wear well over time.

As we try to learn from our own experience and from observing others, let's give our kids some simple, objective ways to determine quality in their perspective employer and have the discipline to walk away from an opportunity that seems appealing in the short term.

If IBM or GE recruited all our kids, we wouldn't need to work through this, but since this is unlikely, here are some discussion points.

1. How long has the average employee been with this company? If the answer is positive, your employer will know and be proud to tell you.

2. Spend just a few dollars to get a Dunn and Bradstreet report on the company. Again, the home office may be impressive and their promotional material first class, but their debt to equity ratio and supplier reports on whether they pay on time is far more telling.

3. Get the names and home phone numbers of one or two employees who have had several years in the company. Call them, introduce yourself and ask if they would be willing to help you gain some insight into the company. Then sit back and listen with all your antennae up.

4. Talk with a competitor in their industry. They'll almost always give you an objective, honest evaluation of both strengths and weaknesses. They'll respect your thorough approach and realize

that as an individual, they need not fear telling you their honest view of the company and maybe even key managers.

In addition to this human wisdom, seek God's wisdom. Ask Him to open the doors that will lead you to His will. Then, once you're satisfied that the color runs all the way through the fabric of your prospective employer, go forward with 110% assurance. Make James 1:5 and Numbers 23:19 your personal motto.

❏ I choose to teach this   Date Completed   _____

_____

_____

Retain Professional Services for any High Value Decision/Action

In other sections of this book, we've discussed the importance of getting the right tool for the job and how short cuts often end up costing more in time, money, headaches and most every other measure of value. If this concept is true for the small daily decisions that have small, daily consequences, how much more is it true for the major investments and actions that can have life long implications?

My favorite example is buying or selling a home. The short cut is to say, "I can sell this $200,000 home myself and save the $12,000 commission. Why give up most of my hard work in appreciating the value of this house to a realtor?" Or as a buyer, "why tie myself to one realtor? I can decide for myself which home to buy and then bargain for the best price."

Both of these statements are fraught with error. Let's consider a few objective benefits a realtor provides to buyers and sellers.

For buyers:
1. In the early years a realtor can show a young person or couple how they could make a prudent investment in a home and begin building equity rather than giving away rent. With professional help, young adults may be able to start earlier than they think.

2. They can provide expertise on all the options relating to mortgages and financing.

3. Everyone knows location is a critical factor in a home's value, and no one knows location like a proven local realtor.

4. Your realtor has access to the Multiple Listing Service to scan through virtually every home in a geographic area in a certain price range.

5. They have usually walked through the home and can see it with your needs and desires in mind.

For sellers:

1. Again, the Multiple Listing Service puts your home in front of hundreds of realtors and prospective buyers.

2. A realtor has contacts with relocation companies to quickly serve qualified buyers from out of town.

3. They can maximize your sell price by knowing every comparable home in the area.

4. At the point of negotiation they are not emotionally involved and the buyer knows it.

5. They can provide the tools and expertise to weed out a financially unqualified buyer before you've wasted 5 weeks and the "signed contract" becomes worthless at the closing table.

6. A realtor will show your house so you don't have to be cordial while strangers turn up their nose at your beloved home.

A similar list could be drawn up with reasons to retain an attorney if you face a significant legal challenge. The financial and long-term consequences of being a lone ranger in a courtroom far outweigh the cost of a reputable attorney.

When your family faces one of these financially significant crossroads, turn to Proverbs 15:22 and take the opportunity to involve your teens in the discussion. They will learn from your resolve and gain confidence from your wisdom.

❏ I choose to teach this   Date Completed   _____

_____

_____

Principle of Margin

Once there were two brothers. The older brother had done very well in his work. He earned over $200,000 most years, but it never seemed to be quite enough. He was often overdrawn at the bank and most troubling of all, he had accumulated a pile of 18% credit card debt that he couldn't seem to pay down. The constant tension and arguments were taking a toll on his marriage, too.

In contrast to all of this, the younger brother worked at a mid level position that paid $62,000 per year. Raises only came as cost of living adjustments. He, however, had no credit card debt and they were making steady progress on their mortgage. (Granted it was 1/5 the size of his older brother's). In their home, the weekends and monthends rarely held a word of tension or arguments over family finances.

Here's how the principle goes: **No matter what your income, plan your family budget, including giving and long-term savings, to equal no more than 95% of your income**. Life's unexpected surprises will often take the last 5%. Many families refuse this kind of personal discipline and make purchases that run closer to 110% or more, of their income. The result, of course, is growing debt as the 10% plus interest expense keeps adding up every year. They are no happier with that additional 15%. In fact, just the opposite is true. Debt causes fear and tension over all things financial, and once you've accepted a 10% family deficit, going to 15% or 20% is an open question, which will only add to the arguments and tension.

Don't take my word for it. Take an honest look at your own family finances. Look at the lives of friends who are in debt even though they take home more income than you. We can all see the truth that there are families living on less, but somehow they aren't accumulating debt and living with the financial tension and arguments. My guess is they are living proof for the principle of margin.

Share this concept with your kids and find examples to dramatize your point. Do it—not because you want to deprive them of what that extra 15-20% could buy, but because you're wise enough to know that a little more is never enough and anything over 100% just brings growing debt, frustration and family quarrels.

❏ I choose to teach this   Date Completed   _____

_____

_____

Sleep with Dogs and You Get Fleas

Samson! The name has become synonymous with physical strength—but certainly not strength of character. Samson; the man who could carry the city gate of his enemies several miles just to make a dramatic statement to them. Safe to say, if your neighbor's dog is named Samson, he probably doesn't need a burglar alarm.

But what else do we know about Samson? If you're familiar with the Biblical story, he started out great. He had good intentions, like most of us. But Samson was unaware that if you get too close to your adversary, too comfortable, it is impossible to avoid being tainted by their disease. If you sleep with dogs, you get fleas. For Samson, it was literally true that he slept and fell in love with Delilah, who eventually betrayed him. The result was that his eyes were gouged out with an iron sword. It's interesting that iron was the high tech metal perfected by the Philistines but not understood yet by Israel in 1100 B.C. It was one of the things Samson so admired about his adversaries.

Like Samson, whenever we choose to align ourselves with someone or something, it will necessarily affect us. No one calls all the shots in a relationship. The employee exercises <u>some</u> autonomy as he represents the company. Your friend makes <u>some</u> contribution to what you do together. Neither marriage partner exerts complete control on the family's activities and reputation.

I'll never forget the first time this principle became evident to me. I was still in my 20's working for a small entrepreneurial company headed by a successful publisher. I had negotiated a partnership—a tag-on to our product that would qualify us to sell to an entirely new market. The other company's reputation in our small industry was poor. I was shocked at several things during our negotiations. But after all, I rationalized, they're supplying us. We are in control of the final product. My boss and I didn't then, and still don't agree on many things, but in this case, he had 30 years of wisdom that I had yet to learn. He simply shook his head and said, "If you sleep with dogs, you get fleas." We walked away from that opportunity at the 11th hour, and surely avoided more pain and trouble than the imagined profits could have balanced.

Sometime when the potential reward is high, but the price is clearly sleeping with dogs, take a strong lead with your son or daughter on this principle.

❏ I choose to teach this   Date Completed   _____
                                                       _____
                                                       _____

Principles of Compromise

(Something vs. Nothing or Moral Absolutes)

When it comes to compromising or giving in on a position we hold, none of us go down easily. We believe our position is truly the wisest course, and besides, there is that painful pride that gets hurt if we compromise.

Let's look at three levels or circumstances that our kids should become familiar with, since all of us, at some time, will find ourselves in each of these three levels.

I. **Level One.** I believe there are **moral absolutes**. If you don't we can't compromise because by definition, moral absolutes are, well, absolute. If Robert Redford offers Woody Harrelson $1,000,000 to sleep with his wife (or mine), I'm sorry; it's an absolute no. The same goes for $2,000,000 or $200,000,000. When people violate absolutes for a price, it doesn't change what is true or false, right or wrong, it just means they chose to violate a moral absolute. It can't be justified, they just did it anyway and sold their convictions.

II. **Level Two.** If we are not in a circumstance where moral absolutes are involved, then is there **an agreed authority structure**? The word "agreed" is critical. If I am subordinate to my boss at work, then excluding moral absolutes, I am obliged to follow his final decisions or leave the firm so that he is no longer my superior. Now, a wise boss, parent or other authority will talk, listen and genuinely hear the opinions of his subordinates. They may provide wisdom and insight he hasn't seen before. He may choose to incorporate many of their ideas in his final decision or he may wisely delegate the entire effort to subordinates and let them sink or swim. In either case, it's really not a compromise as much as it is a consultation. The outcome was never really in doubt in the sense that there is an agreed decision maker. True compromise is level three. This is the area where our emotions and energy are most often focused.

III. **Level Three. Something vs. nothing** among peers. Unless there is an agreed authority structure (level 2), for the purposes of decision making and compromising, we are peers and the issue will be played out at level 3. You may believe you are in authority, but unless both parties are willing to act on your authority, you are peers. At this point it is something vs. nothing. If you and I are truly at a log jam, neither will agree to the other's position, then a wise man will see that he should compromise, get something, and probably put the issue to rest. Can I choose "nothing" and avoid any compromise? Rarely, because the "nothing" option usually leaves the issue on the table unresolved. Every time it is reintroduced, it becomes more painful for everyone and the decision has to be made again and again. In those cases where the decision involves a one time opportunity that will pass, never to be raised again, choosing "nothing" as opposed to "something" is called "throwing the baby out with the bath water".

It is usually stubborn pride on the part of one or both of us that leads to a "nothing" choice as opposed to "something". Rarely is a true moral absolute at the root or we would have disposed of the issue much sooner. Try this diagram along with some french fries with your early teenager. They may not fully appreciate how this will play out for them as parents, spouses, employees, etc., but having a clear understanding of the three levels is a good start.

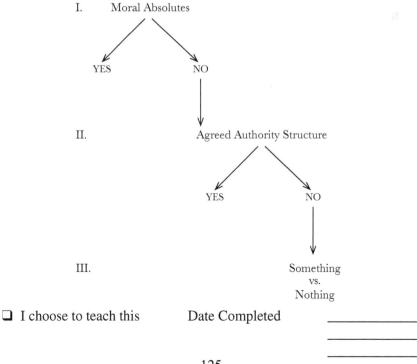

I.   Moral Absolutes

YES   NO

II.   Agreed Authority Structure

YES   NO

III.   Something
                                     vs.
                                  Nothing

❑ I choose to teach this   Date Completed   _____
                                                      _____
                                                      _____

Standing Alone (and the likely consequences)

Several years ago I served on a committee that had to appoint a chairman. It was a paid position and even though the position had a limited term, as a practical matter, whomever filled the slot often did so for many years. With wisdom or not, we had agreed that only a unanimous decision would be acceptable. Right there, the issue of standing alone came into play, for of course, only when others are affected by the one who stands alone, does it have any relevance.

As I rethink that experience and others like it, here are a few approaches that have helped me.

1. In your mind, remove the time factor. Take away the urgency. Picture the situation resulting from a "go" and a "no go" decision. What does the future look like one year or more away? You probably have a better handle on that future vision than most people since you are in a position to be potentially standing alone. Trust your future vision.

2. What does your experience tell you from previous, similar experiences? Oh sure, there are a dozen reasons why you can say this one is different, it will work out well, but that could have been said, and probably was said, in all those previous examples, too.

3. If you're about to stand-alone and significantly affect the outcome, take a hard look at what the others see that you don't. Listen with an open mind. If for no other reason than self protection, if you make the ship go down, you better be very sure you're not wishing you could change your mind one week or one year later. Go back to point #1 above and reconsider all the best reasons your opponents offer.

4. Similar to #1, remove all the gathered momentum around this decision. Others have worked hard to bring the issue to this decision point; many have committed themselves publicly to one view or another. In your mind (better yet on paper), list and summarize

1-3 above, with no weight given to the effort by well-intentioned builders. If it's a good decision, it will stand on its merits without your sympathy vote for those who have worked so hard. If it isn't a good decision, one-month or one year later, it will be blame rather than pressure to go along that you'll be feeling, and the hard work of the supporters will be quickly forgotten in favor of blaming the one(s) who could have stopped it.

It is this final point #4 that can provide the most focus. If in your heart there is a good/less good, best/acceptable choice, it is usually only courage that is needed to realize that there will be another day, another choice, and that standing alone may be the best move instead of taking all the consequences of going the easy road.

❏ I choose to teach this   Date Completed   _____

                                                _____

                                                _____

Career Focus and Building an Area of Expertise

In the summer after my college graduation, while I was earnestly seeking God's complete and specific will for the next fifty years of my life, a wise counselor told me "…just do something worthwhile, and if it doesn't work out, do something else, but do something." He saw in me a greater danger of paralysis, (that is, not doing anything for fear of not doing the right thing) more than the risk of doing something worthless.

At first it sounded like weak advice, but unless you have unusual certainty for the future, a 22-year-old liberal arts graduate would do well to "do something worthwhile." It is good advice to become exposed to many possible career paths and then begin to focus as your interests, training and natural talents are recognized. In my case, it was within the general field of business and sales. I knew that much but what industry or area of expertise; only time would tell.

As your son or daughter begins to ponder their future, offer the funnel advice: start broad and over time, focus a career as skills are recognized. It is important to talk about this two, three, or maybe four years before graduation, before the sense of panic or the allure of a very focused opportunity may cloud the wisdom you can offer.

The flip side of this principle applies to some of us and our kids will be twice blessed if they hear it from you first. That is, once you're past the first few years of entry-level positions, make a conscious commitment toward long-term consistency in your career. See your talents for their real worth and then apply them in your industry or field. A 40-year-old executive with almost twenty years in his industry is a skilled and valuable asset. When the need or opportunity comes to move along, how will he be viewed next to the candidate whose track record shows five or six false starts in different fields?

Start broad then focus by design. There will be temptations to violate both of these goals, but I believe that on balance, our sons and daughters will do well if they try first to apply this approach, having learned it from you.

❏ I choose to teach this   Date Completed   _____

_____

_____

128

Shooting the Messenger

"Don't shoot the messenger". We've all been told how this reaction does no good, (especially for the messenger). It would be worthwhile to address even this obvious principle considering how many of us, too often, see only the moment and vent our reaction on someone who has absolutely no control over the circumstance. He is only a "messenger".

But right there is the key to a response that is appropriate and effective. If there is a legitimate problem, take the moment to determine how you can create a desire in the "controller" to act on your behalf. Is it a simple appeal to his good will? Is it that you're a "customer" by some definition and you, therefore, hold some power over him? (This, by the way, is less effective than you might imagine.) Or is it the best of all worlds where you can show the controller how it is both in your interests, and his, for him to respond to your wishes and viewpoint. How to frame this issue and motivate the controller is another discussion, but the point of this principle is first to pause long enough in our moment of turmoil to identify when we are dealing only with an innocent messenger. Then, to determine who the real controller is and whether it is worth any effort to try to affect a change.

Note: The messenger will almost certainly expect your negative response if he bears bad news. How surprised will he be and how much respect and appreciation will be gained for you, if you offer calm words of acceptance and understanding that, after all, "he's just the messenger?"

For this principle to meaningfully connect with your kids, you can't just decide to discuss "messengers" and "controllers" on your next date night. First, you need to be aware of it yourself and when a real life opportunity presents itself in front of your children, offer calm words of understanding to a messenger instead of the natural frustrated response. A day or two later, while it is still clear in everyone's mind, talk about it together.

❏ I choose to teach this   Date Completed   _____

_____

_____

Steno Pad – The Simple Daily File Manager

What was the name of that business prospect that called our office? I think it was in early April last year. And what was his phone number? And the price the lumberyard quoted me for mulch last year – I know they were the best price but what was it? And, I need to remind myself to cancel this trial subscription next June 10th or I'll automatically get charged $49.95.

Do all these things sound familiar? Of course. They are simple, real life details that will fall through the cracks unless we have a simple daily organizational tool.

This practical tool was introduced to me when I was 22, sitting in a two-week training course in my first job. One of the people who talked with us shared that the steno pad was the most effective daily filing system he had ever found. He was still using it after many years. Today, years later, I can tell you I'd be lost without my steno pad in my briefcase.

Take a standard flip top steno pad. Mark today's date on the first page, the next day on the 2nd page until all the pages are dated. One book will last 2-3 months. Then mark the cover as book #1 and write in the start/end dates. Now use one page per day as your detail/scratch pad for key phone calls, numbers, names, prices, your short to-do list, etc. If you're like me, you'll want to remind yourself to do something one week, or one month from today. Flip forward to that date, write the shorthand reminder to yourself, and then relax. You'll never forget an important follow-up responsibility. At the end of one year, you'll have about four well worn pads and the ability to quickly retrieve the details from a day six or nine months earlier.

This isn't intended to be a calendar to manage your appointments, or a business management software tool, nor is it a time management or strategic planning tool. (For a strategic planning tool to help us determine the most important things and how to organize to accomplish them, I know of no better tool than Stephen Covey's Q1-Q4 concept and the weekly planning guide divided into our life roles.) Rather, the flip pad is a record and a reminder of today's details that become so valuable when you have them and so frustrating when they can't be found. Admittedly, this system will work best for someone whose job is geared toward the phone, desk and ongoing projects. It's less useful if your work is prescribed for you. Of all the umpteen time management / self help tools being offered, this is one that I will pass along to my boys. When something continues as a part of your daily habit for almost thirty years, it must be working.

❑ I choose to teach this   Date Completed   _____

_____

_____

Choose a Church Carefully, Then Stick with it Over the Years

When I buy toothpaste, I'm only a customer. There is no benefit or loss if I switch brands every time. Some people treat their church involvement a lot like buying toothpaste – a simple consumer decision – what's best for me and my family – right now.

This principle is rooted in a more basic question: Why do we choose and participate in a church in the first place? Right thinking about this question will help bring the issue into focus.

Why do we join a church?

1. To participate with other believers in worship.

2. To learn the truths of Scripture.

3. To build friendships with other Christians and enjoy those relationships.

4. To love and give to meet the needs of others.

5. To mature and become more Christ-like in our daily lives.

6. To rear children in the fear and love of the Lord. This is not to be confused with leading them to make a personal commitment to Christ. This is primarily the responsibility and joy of parents, but the church should be a great help in teaching and training. Your church should be a place where your kids grow up with love and familiarity, participating with you even before they fully understand that the Church is God's invention, not man's, that it is His chosen instrument to affect the world.

7. To serve in the area where God has given you particular talent and ability whether it be teaching, evangelism, care giving to those in need, general administrative leadership, etc.

For those who would seek to be part of the general spiritual and administrative leadership, it can take years to earn the credibility and platform from which to lead effectively. If you throw in the towel every few years and switch to what appears to be greener pastures, you may be depriving yourself and your church of your own talents and skills. But more relevant to our subject here, as your children observe your life, you may be depriving them of the opportunity to learn the long term value of staying with a church family through thick and thin and sharing in the benefits of that commitment.

❏ I choose to teach this   Date Completed   _____

_____

_____

Leadership vs. Management

Good management is often mistaken for effective leadership. At the same time, both are essential to the progress of any organization, business, church or family. Management is the ability to take a plan and run with it. Leadership knows which plan to choose. Management can win the battle, but leadership must first decide if the battle is worth winning. Management will plan, budget and pull off your family vacation. Leadership must decide if, and when your family needs a vacation in the context of the past twelve months and the coming twelve months.

This is not intended to make light of the management role. Again, both are essential. Many leaders are notoriously bad managers. They have the right vision and can motivate their troops toward the goal, but if it were left up to them, it would stop there.

In God's plan, husbands and fathers are to be leaders. Always thinking and looking ahead one month, one year, five years, in order to set those directions today that will take the family to the right destination way down the road. Imagine how wasteful it would be for a father to take his family on vacation, managing the trip well, safely navigating through traffic and keeping to a balanced budget, with no particular destination in mind. He managed well, but there was no leadership.

Let me suggest three essentials for effective leadership.

An effective leader must:

1. Have a healthy dissatisfaction with things as they are.

2. Have a clear vision of things as they should (could) be.

3. Have the courage to move/lead against the pull of things as they are.

It is important to realize that every leader, not most, but every leader will encounter resistance to his leadership. That's because he is, by definition, moving people away from the status quo, and most people are more comfortable with the familiar than with the unknown.

Talk about these three essentials with your teen when, together, you have seen and felt the effect of particularly strong or weak leadership.

❑ I choose to teach this   Date Completed   _____

_____

_____

Circles of Responsibility

Do you remember the formula for the area of a circle? On a school night, give your 17-year-old a surprise homework break. Go have an ice cream together and ask him/her the same question.

As we all grow into adulthood, the expanding responsibilities (and their associated privileges) are a lot like concentric circles.

THE EXPANDING RESPONSIBILITIES AND PRIVILEGES OF ADULTHOOD

The smallest, inner circle might represent a boy—not very much responsibility required at this level. But as that boy grows and goes off to college, significant responsibility is placed on his shoulders. His response—whether he carries those new responsibilities or squanders them—directly affects his ability to move into the next circle, a career.

And so it goes. A measure of demonstrated responsibility at the career level is necessary for a young man to successfully move to the next circle—a marriage. A solid marriage (tested over time) is the foundation for successfully navigating an even larger circle—a family. Finally, a public ministry, beyond your own family is the final circle. That ministry may be a small discipleship group, church leadership, community leadership, organizational leadership through a board of directors, or a visible national ministry. Regardless, the principle remains that significant failure on any of the inner circles will imperil our ability to serve effectively at the next level. Each of these circles, in their proper time and place, are stepping-stones to the next. Ignoring the connection and assuming we can hopscotch life's natural progression, or compartmentalize our lives, is a formula for collapse.

Equally so, once a person has arrived at a certain level, a humble recognition of our dependence on our inner circles honors the Lord and protects us from prideful failure. The leader of a national (or local) ministry, who fails to tend to his family, is on thin ice. The father who fails to nurture his marriage is eroding the foundation of that family, etc.

But now lets come back to your 17-year-old and the discussion over ice cream. Paint this picture from a positive viewpoint. Use these circles to bring a positive vision of adulthood that he can strive toward, and the unavoidable formula for achieving and sustaining it. Give him a picture, with definition and focus, on a subject that he generally understands, but where he has never seen the connection between the circles.

In our family, I copied this illustration and spent $3.00 at Kinko's to have it laminated as a wallet card. Make the same effort yourself and give it to your son or daughter. Ask them to keep it in their wallet until they can pass it on to their 17-year-old. In I Corinthians 13:11, Paul says: *"When I was a child, I talked like a child, I thought like a child, I reasoned like a child, but when I became a man, I put childish ways behind me."*

Note: Somewhere in the discussion, after they have given you the formula for the area of a circle, do the math together and point out that just as a 2" circle has an area of 3", and a 3" circle has an area of 7", and a 4" circle has an area of 13", so it is that each jump to the next level in our life circles vastly increases the size of our responsibility compared to the previous circle.

❑ I choose to teach this   Date Completed   _____

_____

_____

General Skills And Knowledge

The glory of young men is their strength,
of old men, their experience.
Proverbs 20:29

Learning to Drive in Stages, Starting at Age 6 or 7

Driving from your lap at a very early age in a safe, empty parking lot is a good start. As soon as they have their permit or license, however, give them real opportunity and training in at least three areas.

1. **On an icy, slick day, use the opportunity to find a vacant parking lot and teach control of a car on ice.**

   Most anyone can safely drive in good weather, but when they're driving home from college through a Midwestern snowstorm, you'll be glad they have already handled 30 or 40 icy skids.

2. **Two-lane passing.**

   In the spring of 1996, I was on a business trip with three other men that required us to drive through rural Missouri. We were running late, so as we were able, we passed several cars. A young couple in a '65 Mustang also seemed to be rushing and you might guess the rest of the story. As we approached a ravine, we pulled back in since the line of sight was not clear over the knoll and down the hill. Sure enough, a pickup emerged from that small depression and as it approached, in a moment's time, we all realized the Mustang was committed to passing us. We pulled into the ditch but it was no help. The pickup and Mustang impacted with tremendous force just beside our driver's door. The injuries I saw that day would make any father resolve to teach this skill carefully.

   Try this approach. Sit in the left rear seat behind your licensed son or daughter so you can both see and judge the oncoming traffic. Select an appropriate two-lane highway and as you drive, talk through the judgment decisions of distance, speed, hills and corners. Pass at least 10-15 times and repeat the process at night when your confidence is there. This most dangerous element of driving can only be mastered through practice, so you take the responsibility to provide the safety net as your kids learn this form of tightrope walking.

3. **Driving a stick.**

   Sooner or later we all are faced with driving a stick shift. A few lurches and stalls and the skill can be learned. This is an opportunity to take your young driver to an open parking lot on their 14th or 15th birthday – long before they would expect it – and teach them this basic skill. It will be the highlight of their birthday and another victory for father/child identification.

❑ I choose to teach this   Date Completed   _____

_____

_____

Reading a Map with a Compass

Around age 9 or 10, learning to use a map and compass together can be an enjoyable, valuable learning experience, and like so many others, will result in a growing bond between you and your kids.

Take a map of any terrain that has identifiable landmarks. The area needs to be large enough so that finding your way out will require a little time and effort. A golf course is one possibility. A better option might be a forest preserve – so long as you can get a simple map of the area. Walk or drive into the area having a compass and your map with you. Go to a landmark on the map such as a lake or a meadow. The top of your map will always be north, the bottom south, etc. Place the compass in the center of the map. Then turn your map as necessary so that the compass needle points to the top of the map. Your map is now true to the world. From there you can walk to other landmarks on the map, repeating this process until you reach your objective.

Once you have completed this adventure, don't miss the opportunity to discuss a spiritual truth. God's Word is our spiritual compass in life. It tells us what is true and what is false just like a compass tells which way north really is regardless of whether you or I may think north is another direction. So it is that in life, our friends may decide to try drugs, sex, or wasting time just hanging out, thinking it is the way to grow up and get where they want to go. And who can blame them? They don't have a spiritual compass. So they go the wrong way, through very dangerous terrain. We, on the other hand, can trust the Bible to be our guide just like we trust a compass to show us true north, south, east, and west.

All kids want to be successful, growing up to be happy, productive adults. The only question is whether they'll trust their compass for life.

This whole experience, and the principle, can be reinforced if, at a high stakes moment of choice, usually in early adolescence, you give your child a real compass, engraved with "Psalm 119:105". But make sure you've already done the compass adventure together.

❏ I choose to teach this   Date Completed   _____
                                                          _____
                                                          _____

Manners and Their Importance

You may have heard about the boy who was so full of energy that he kept standing at the dinner table. In an effort to teach at least some manners, his father insisted he sit down. It became a repeated nightly battle until one night the father threatened that if he didn't sit down he would go to his room with no supper. The boy sat down but was heard to mumble under his breath, "I'm standing up on the inside."

When I think of manners in the context of children and of our boys in particular, one seemingly insignificant event sticks in my mind. Colson was 9 and we were running a quick trip to the grocery store together. In the parking lot a good friend whom I hadn't seen for months honked and I knew we would meet in the store. I took the next moment to remind Colson that this was an opportunity to do those three things we had talked about before:

1. Look up, straight into their eyes.

2. Extend his right hand, and

3. Say, "Nice to meet you."

For pre-teens especially, this is sure to result in a positive, "What a fine young man" kind of statement from the adult. Just enough to reinforce the courage that it takes when a young child is just starting to voluntarily interact with adults outside their home.

The main point here is found in the story of the boy who was standing on the inside. We may succeed at forcing a whole etiquette book of manners on our kids only to have them rebel against it later when the issues should have long since become non-issues. The key is for our kids to believe in the importance of manners more than being force fed a long list of the manners themselves. Children want to be highly regarded and respected just like the rest of us, and receiving admiration and respect from adults is the strongest motivation toward good manners. One or two areas like the handshake, specifically taught and practiced, will provide the response that will help motivate our children to observe and repeat other manners.

After that encounter in the grocery store, Colson looked up and said, "Well Dad, did I get it?" He knew the answer, but my enthusiastic response made him feel like he had won a blue ribbon. After a success and recognition experience like that, it's easier, even for a 9 year old, to believe that manners in general are important. Once that bridge is crossed, the specific manners themselves will come naturally all in good time.

❏ I choose to teach this   Date Completed   _____

                                                      _____

                                                      _____

" Hey Dad, Can You Pound a Nail Straight?"

Chances are if you can, it's because your father could too. We know that for better or worse, our kids will repeat most of the patterns they observe in us. When it comes to sealing the wood deck, grouting and caulking around the shower, wallpapering or hanging a new light fixture, do you do it yourself or head for the yellow pages? If we are comfortable with these projects, it's probably because we helped our dad, or got in his way, when we were kids. So here's the important point. Go the extra mile to let your little "helpers" be there at your side when you're doing a project. Their attention span will be short when they are too young to be of any real help, but by the time they are teenagers, some quality time can be had together working on a project. The tools in our hands can be the means towards building the relationship with them. And remember, rules without relationship leads to rebellion.

My personal view is never to insist that they participate but rather make it a positive experience to be with you. Some boys or girls have a natural bent toward working with their hands and take real joy in a project accomplished. If one of yours is built that way, take advantage of it. Build a deck or finish a basement for the sake of you and your son/daughter. Never mind whether you really need a finished basement, your real goal is much more valuable.

❏ I choose to teach this   Date Completed   _____

_____

_____

144

Music

A philosopher once said: "Music, math and literature – teach these three and you'll lack nothing in a well rounded education." I heard another philosopher say, "The only instrument I can play is the radio and even that ends up being country and western".

Our kids do not need to become virtuosos, but music is such a uniquely powerful part of the human experience that we do them a great service if we give them the ability to play more than the radio.

When God made man in His image, it included our unique ability to make and appreciate music. Scripture says that the morning stars sang together in praise of God's creation. Heaven is often described as a place where saints and angels will sing praises to God. David, the most musical of the Biblical writers, praised God by saying "You have put a new song in my mouth, a song of praise unto our God."

Developing this part of our God given nature – music – is a key that opens a whole panorama of joy and appreciation in our kids. Who enjoys the symphony more? Likely the one who has had at least beginner's training on an instrument. Who can sing along with his voice and heart and experience tears of joy? More often it is the one who has grown up singing in school and church choirs. They can be moved because they know from experience the rich and rewarding sounds that come only from practice and long hours of training.

Some might say, what good are the costly music lessons if it never amounts to more than a few band concerts? For me, learning to read music, gaining some level of skill and an appreciation for excellent performance – this is the key that opens up the joy of participating in and receiving music as adults.

What would life be if we couldn't read? All written communication would be closed to us. Similarly, if the sum of our kid's musical skill is playing the radio, they will not be able to fully experience a wonderful part of what God has built into us.

❏ I choose to teach this   Date Completed   _____

_____

_____

You Be There to Teach your Child to Ride a Bike

Can you remember when you first learned to ride a bike? Can you remember who was there? Was it a cold day with a new Christmas gift or maybe a summer afternoon with your older brother? If you're like me, you can remember each of these details, and guess what, so will your kids. So don't miss the opportunity to be the central character in this childhood event that they'll always remember.

But there is something else. After you have run beside them, and repeatedly caught them on the way down to the pavement, you'll finally achieve the point where they can go it alone. They'll be proud and so will you. So take that teachable moment to hold them and briefly explain that God, our Heavenly Father, does much the same thing for us. He protects us and helps us. He knows when we need a close hand even though we might feel like showing off.

Remember Isaiah 41:10 "So do not fear for I am with you. Do not be dismayed for I am your God. I will strengthen you and help you. I will uphold you with my righteous right hand."

Then take a rest, you'll need it.

❑ I choose to teach this   Date Completed   _____

_____

_____

The 3-4-5 Right Triangle

It's a simple geometry axiom. You probably learned it in 8 th grade as the Pythagorean Theorem. But with a name like that it's no wonder that everyone, except the mechanical engineers, forgot it. It really is useful, though, for camping, building a deck, laying out a garden or doing anything else that you would like to be square.

The 8th grade version works like this: $A^2 + B^2 = C^2$ where A and B are the legs of a right triangle and C is the long edge.

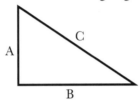

But a simpler way to say the same thing is the 3-4-5 triangle:

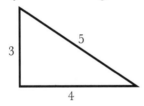

It doesn't matter whether it is 3 feet, 3 yards, or 3 lengths of the same piece of string, so long as the standard is the same. Involve your 9 or 10 year old and use this approach to make your volleyball court or campsite or garden square. They will learn and remember a practical application and think you're pretty smart.

❑ I choose to teach this   Date Completed   _____

_____

_____

Changing a Tire (in the dark)

Rather than a mundane task for them to observe, make changing a tire part of that great rite of passage called "getting their license". Make it a prerequisite before taking the car, that they be able to do the whole job alone with only headlights, a flashlight, or better yet, a road flair. The nighttime test will be fun and will help remove the fear and danger if they face the real thing.

In our family's experience, this event was especially enjoyable. We had already practiced this task once in a warm, well-lighted garage, but when it came time for the "solo tire change test" it happened on a cold winter night (all the better to duplicate the potential real experience). It was a dark (but safe) parking lot. We had already discussed that in case of a real change; they needed to get the car off the road to a safe spot, even if that meant ruining the flat tire.

So using the safety tools already in the trunk (see page 160) he began the job. The first problem arose with the night flair. This was new. How to light it? He tried striking it like a match on the pavement, to no avail. But then, of course, use the cigarette lighter. One touch and it flared up.

In about 20 minutes, the job was done and we were off for a cup of hot chocolate, both having a higher sense of confidence in his driving alone in the months and years to come.

Dads, let me add one more factor in this discussion, particularly if you have a son. When our boys are on a date with a young lady, they are accepting responsibility for her. Give your son and the girls' parents the assurance that a flat tire will not be an unknown or dangerous event, should it ever happen.

❏ I choose to teach this   Date Completed   _____

_____

_____

Two-Step When You Dance, But Three-Step When You Talk

Of all the skills and training our kids might learn, few things will be more practical over their entire career than the ability to communicate effectively to an audience. Whether it's only to their boss, a small group of peers or a keynote address at a trade show, much of the heart pounding fear will be tamed if our kids know the simple 3-step approach for almost any presentation.

1. **Tell them what you're going to tell them.**
    Take a few brief moments to give the main topics or issues that you'll be addressing. Doing this will force you to organize the talk into logical pieces that fit together.

2. **Tell them**
    This is the body, where you go back to the start and simply touch on each point, as you promised you would, giving all the detail you have time for.

3. **Tell them what you told them.**
    Always plan to finish step 2 with enough time to go back and say "Now let's review what we have covered." Then briefly touch each high point again from the beginning.

Your audience of 1 or 1000 will follow you and remember what you said, and in the process your own confidence will be evident for all to see.

❏ I choose to teach this   Date Completed   _____

_____

_____

Fires and Barbecues – With No Gas Jet.

From the time I was 7 until my college years, our family vacationed every summer at Dore Lake in Northern Saskatchewan, Canada. It was 90 miles of gravel north of the nearest town and electricity and phones were only reluctantly accepted in the late 80's. A small group of families had banded together in the early 60's, deciding to build cabins on this lake where the ice went out in late May and you could still fish with daylight at 10 PM.

This was no Hilton Towers experience. Instead, every day was an adventure as we did all the necessary tasks besides water-skiing, fishing and having shore lunches on far away islands. Those shore lunches were often a feast of fresh fish, potatoes and wild berries. It was dad's job to build the fire just hot enough to handle lunch for eight to ten people. If it had rained the night before, well, with our dad we never considered the possibility that it would prevent the necessary fire.

You may be a camping family, or you may only choose to face a fireplace, but this is one more opportunity for your kids to identify with you, learning a skill that will always be associated with their dad.

The same is true for backyard barbecues. Some dads can make this into an art form. That is another subject, but for our discussion here, it's not the end result that is so important, rather the means of getting there that holds real power for creating a bond with your children.

These skills aren't the kind of thing you teach on some specified day, instead, just let them be a part of it, lighting the match or piling the charcoal, knowing that with their help, it will take longer and make more mess.

There is no test or point of completion for this skill, only another opportunity to create one more small connection to you and all that you stand for.

❏ I choose to teach this   Date Completed   _____

_____

_____

Get the Right Tool for the Job

I enjoy a building project or completing some small repair on my tool bench in the basement. But if you're like me, we'll never have the time or money to acquire and use all the specialized tools you see on those Saturday afternoon building shows. I can see it now. Norm builds an Early American bedroom set in half an hour with the help of his $2,000,000 workshop. Well, that's a little extreme, but here's the principle.

Don't try to build the Early American bedroom set unless you're prepared to buy the $2,000,000 workshop.

There's nothing worse than attempting a level 10 home improvement with level 3 tools. Even Norm would botch the job under those circumstances. And worst of all, the poor quality results advertise themselves and their builder to everyone who enters your door.

A couple years ago, Lora Sue convinced me to wallpaper the kitchen and to include chair rail molding. Sounds easy enough, but after one or two 45° corner cuts by hand, I realized I needed a chop saw with a finish cut blade or this was going to look awful. I borrowed one, and although I wasted a little more lumber than a good carpenter would have, the right tool still gave me a result that made us both proud.

Three things come to mind that relate to this subject:

1. Safety. The wrong tool is never safe.

2. Shortcuts end up taking longer and costing more in the long run since you'll probably have to get the right tool and do it over.

3. For most of us weekend repairmen, a good power tool will last most of a lifetime if it's used and stored in the manner it was built for.

This isn't something you'll need to talk about much. Our kids will automatically repeat what they see us do in this area. Remember that every repair or project you take on will silently advertise the man who built it. So unless you can buy or borrow the $2,000,000 workshop, don't attempt the Early American bedroom set.

❏ I choose to teach this   Date Completed   _____

_____

_____

Three C's for Understanding the Bible

"My understanding of scripture is different than yours. We can both find a verse to support whatever view we want." We've all heard that opinion expressed and it's true, if you look at the Bible as a grab-bag of unrelated verses. But God didn't intend for His Word to be haphazard doctrine able to be twisted to fit men's opinions. The fact is that when sound methods are used, the Bible will shape our opinions.

Offer your kids the three C's for understanding the Bible. There are college courses more that could be learned on this subject, but this will be a good start toward effective Bible study on their own.

1. Context. Read what comes before and follows after the particular verse. What was the writer trying to say in general to his audience? Was his statement intended for illustration or to be taken literally? The context will shed light on the intended meaning.

2. Comparison. The Bible is still the best commentary on the Bible. Use a cross-reference study Bible to read other passages that speak to the same issue. If the scripture intends to say one thing here, it will always be supported elsewhere. If I can't find any other support or I find contradictory teaching elsewhere, I can be sure I don't have a correct understanding of the original passage.

3. Culture. What were the people thinking when they first received this scripture? What were their needs, mindset, fears, frame of reference and history? Try to see it through their eyes and often a new and meaningful understanding will open up to us.

This is basic, to be sure, but the sad truth is that if our kids will utilize only these three "C's", they will be ahead of most adults in their ability to accurately understand the Bible.

An excellent book that puts this subject in laymen's terms is "Living By The Book," Howard and William Hendrichs, Moody Press, 1991.

❏ I choose to teach this   Date Completed   _____

_____

_____

152

Hidden Keys for Obvious Reasons

When our boys were young we decided to get a conversion van in spite of its increased cost. Being able to drive long distances with a happy, contented and rested family can be worth a lot, especially if you make your purchase decision at the end of a big trip in a small sedan.

So there it was, our new van. First night in the garage. Both keys on the same ring, right from the dealership. I was going to take Lora for a ride, but it was cold out, so I started the engine, slammed the door and let it warm up for a few minutes. We came out to find that our new vehicle automatically locked when you started the engine. So right in the garage we got to test the roadside assistance service instead of the new van.

Hidden keys seem like a simple rule to make for yourself, but how many of us never get around to it. Getting locked out of a car or a house can be inconvenient, costly, and in some cases dangerous. Do it for yourself now and your teen's first car. A magnet case on an inside fender or a ring under the grill seems like a trivial issue until your son and his date are one of the last cars in the parking lot, and far from the nearest 24-hour tow truck.

❑ I choose to teach this   Date Completed   _____

_____

_____

The Family Filing System

Remember the vacation you took two years ago? Of course you do, it was great! I bet you still have the gift certificate the hotel manager gave you for a free stay after the power went out that night. No? Lost hotel and vacation information may be just a minor inconvenience, but the letter your dad wrote you after your first child was born, or the insurance and closing documents on your house, these are priceless. We wouldn't consider running a business without files, but many families live with constant frustration, lost time and lost money because they don't have family files.

Enough said. Here is a partial list that you can pass along when your kids leave home. College isn't too early, but it becomes essential the day they start living in their own residence.

Suggested files:

Federal Taxes: Throughout the year, drop in any statement, or documents you know you'll be needing next April.

Car: Insurance, major repairs, warranties relating to one vehicle.

Projects you manage: Volunteer work, church retreats, etc. Give each a separate file.

Vacations: All the planning, costs, reservations in one place.

Church: Keep a copy of the constitution and annual budgets.

Teaching notes: Do you teach a class at work, church, or school? Keep your hard earned prepared notes forever. You'll likely be asked to teach again.

Investments: Account numbers, quarterly statements, etc.

Medical expenses/receipts: One file per year.

Building: Remodeling projects.

Annual family budgets: Keep previous years budgets in one file.

Personal Resume: Keep updated.

Family/personal credit report: Know how TRW, Experian and Equifax view your credit history. You can be sure your bank and credit card company know.

Any major purchase: Car, boat, house.

College: For each child.

Warranties: For any high ticket purchase.

The list can go on, but the point is to give your kids the gift of an organized household. So literally, give them this gift. Sometime during college or as part of a wedding gift, give then a 2 or 4 drawer metal file cabinet, a hundred blank file folders and share with them an experience of your own when your file cabinet was your best friend.

❑ I choose to teach this   Date Completed   _____

_____

_____

CPR, the Heimlich Maneuver and Basic First Aid

Basic knowledge and skills in first aid are important for two reasons. The most obvious is to help the one who is injured. Our basic training can make the difference between saving a life or standing helplessly by, watching a situation become critical or even fatal. Worse yet, without training, our good intentions can cause more harm than good, creating increased trauma for the victim and liability problems for ourselves.

The second reason is the benefit it brings to the one trained. It provides a measure of personal confidence and a level head when others easily panic or make rash decisions at a trauma scene. Equally important as knowing how to help, is knowing our own limits – knowing where good judgment ends and foolish heroism begins.

Especially as your teens turn 16 and begin driving alone, the incidence of auto accidents or other circumstances with injury are increased. First aid knowledge, skill and a level head are valuable assets at those times. Like most other optional skills and learning, this is one thing that WON'T happen by accident. So you be the one to see that your family is trained in first aid.

Your local YMCA or Red Cross chapters are good places to start. If your kids are in their early teens, why not take the course as a family? Now there's a change of pace that beats the school – TV – homework triangle.

❑ I choose to teach this   Date Completed   _____

_____

_____

156

You Talk With Your Kids About Sex, AIDS & STDs.

When our first son turned 8, I told him that in a few days, he and I were going to have a private talk – somewhere by ourselves – about girls and boys, moms and dads, and where babies come from. Then I went straight to Lora Sue for help. I really did and together we discussed how best to approach it. And so, armed with our ideas and what I had read about this part of fathering, Colson and I picked up some McDonalds and went to a familiar spot that had no possibility of distractions or interruptions. What followed was over an hour of simple, but honest communication about sex. As a bi-product, it was a big step towards a more trusting relationship.

Our goal as dads should be to have this talk (it will end up being several talks over time) before they hear false, twisted, perverted or partial information from older peers. If we come at it too late, their innocence is partially lost and we'll have to undo false or twisted concepts.

Separate from the initial talk, perhaps years later when they are just beginning to face the subject of sexual activity among peers, have a very frank, informed discussion of AIDS and sexually transmitted diseases. Do your research. One phone call to Focus on the Family (1-800-AFAMILY) or other qualified source will give you enough information to do the job well. Focus' video series "Life on the Edge" is a professional approach for a youth group or home setting.

For older teens, explain that as of 2007, according to the Center for Disease Control*, 30 million Americans over the age of 12 have human papilloma virus (HPV). Often, these people are unaware, or ignore the symptoms hoping they will just go away with time. As a result of this virus, many women will eventually contract cervical cancer. Think about it. If you subtract out all of the faithful parents and other adults who are not sexually promiscuous, imagine how high the incidence is among teens. Explain how a condom is no sure prevention and that only one failure is necessary for contracting the communicable disease or a pregnancy, since other forms of contraception are likely avoided if a condom is a trusted choice. Make it clear that abstinence is the only sure way to avoid all of these. Discuss the fact that, no matter what they might say, if your partner is promiscuous enough to have contact with <u>you</u> before marriage, they've

157

likely had, or will have contact with others who can easily be disease carriers.

Finally, bring the discussion to a spiritual level. For those of us who are Christians, redeemed and bought by Christ, he has a vested interest in shaping us into the image of his Son. The world, which has rejected Christ, is another matter, but God will not stand idly by while we disgrace His name and move away from a Christ-like lifestyle. He won't force His will, but the consequences (there is that word again) of flagrant disobedience can be long, painful, and in the context of this discussion, physical.

*CDC.gov/std

❑ I choose to teach this   Date Completed   _____

_____

_____

Who does the Laundry?

This is one of those skills that fall under the category of "They'll learn it themselves – someday." You can accomplish a couple of worthwhile objectives, however, if you choose to tackle this one, and have some fun in the process.

Here's an idea: Start by making part of the job a component in their weekly chores – tied to any allowance they earn. This can be separating the clothes by darks and whites or folding the clean clothes and putting them away – everyone's, not just their own. As they get older, go through the washer/dryer task together and agree that for a while, their jeans (or some other durable item) are their own responsibility. Take the opportunities presented rather than trying to force your own. When there is a certain shirt that <u>has</u> to be ready for a certain date, you have a motivated opportunity to introduce them to a steam iron.

There is no reason to have a crash course in basic laundry the week before your teen heads off to college. If they learn it years ahead of that time they will have earned a measure of self-confidence and independence and you'll have made a statement to them on the value and worth of the homemaker in your family.

❑ I choose to teach this   Date Completed   _____

_____

_____

Preventative Maintenance, Safety Gear and Tools Related to the Car

I was 19 and for the first time was away at college with my own car. Changing the oil in those days was a job you did yourself, so feeling very responsible, I drove into the college physical plant lot and started the job. I was unable to loosen the oil pan nut, however, so I asked one of the engineers to see if he could get it off. From under the car he began to laugh. He said, "Son, you've been pulling on the transmission fluid nut. If you had gotten it off, you'd have drained the transmission fluid, added 4 more quarts of oil and driven out of here."

We have to do it anyway, so the next time you go in for an oil change or to have the brake pads replaced, take your younger kids along. Let them see how to pull the right plug, where the oil goes and the costly damage that is done when worn pads tear into disc brakes. When it comes to safety gear and tools, let them be a part of your task as you make sure your car has the basics:

1. A night flair

2. A tow rope

3. Jumper cables

4. A small shovel and ice scraper in winter (if you live in the snow)

5. Tire changing equipment (jack and spare)

6. Hand spotlight (not necessary but a big help at an accident scene.)

7. A flashlight

With this basic equipment, most any situation will be safer, quicker, and cheaper than if you don't have tools. Then when they get their first car, go with them to get the supplies. Learning to use them should be a required part of getting their driver's license (see p.139).

All of this is the kind of thing that for the most part will be caught, not taught. If you are constantly paying for repairs or find yourself ill equipped to help a stranded motorist, don't expect your kids to be naturally responsible with their own cars.

❏ I choose to teach this   Date Completed   _____

_____

_____

Financial Principles

Be sure you know the condition of your flocks,
give careful attention to your herds;
for riches do not endure forever,
and a crown is not secure for all generations.
Proverbs 27:23

Loaning and Collecting Money

I was only 19, and the experience is one I'll never forget. My older brother had loaned $4,000 to his close friend, Jack. This is no small amount even now, but at the time, it was even more significant. It was a short-term loan for a specific need. They had drawn up a notarized promissory note detailing the schedule for full repayment. My job was simple. While my brother was out of town, I was to meet Jack and receive the full payment on the specific date.

You could probably finish the story. That day came and went with a reasonable excuse. But as many days passed, even this naïve college boy saw that the money was never going to be repaid. All of the verbal promises and notarized documents couldn't force one dollar of repayment. I learned an inexpensive lesson. My brother's learning cost him a healthy sum for a young man just starting out.

First, let me state the principle as I see it. **Never make a personal loan unless you are prepared to make it a free gift.**

This may seem straight forward enough, but how can we make sure our kids don't have to learn this one the hard way.

1. Tell my story, or one of your own, to dramatize this principle. When their "friend" presents a dire and believable need, a true story will come to mind easier than an abstract principle.

2. Explain how all of the documentation is only as good as your ability to collect. Do a role-play or a dialog to ask what recourse they will actually have if their friend doesn't pay. Trace the course of a subpoena, court, a judgment against someone with little or no assets and speculate at your own legal costs to take it that far.

3. Ask whether a person who finds himself in short term financial trouble is really a good credit risk.

4. No amount of short-term interest promised is worth it if neither the principle nor the interest is repaid.

Considering that you may have to get financially involved yourself if it is your son or daughter who learns this lesson the hard way, isn't it to everyone's best interest if they learn this one early, the easy way?

❑ I choose to teach this   Date Completed   _____

_____

_____

Giving Back to the Lord Before Satisfying Our Desires or Funding Our Own Long Term Savings

See Proverbs 3:9, 10   II Corinthians 9:6

1. This principle is never an excuse to be delinquent on our obligations, but to structure our financial house on the remaining funds after giving to the Lord. All too often, the exact opposite of this is the approach we take when deciding our charitable giving.

2. Show your kids how to set up a separate checking account used to hold and disperse the Lord's money only. Make that deposit the first check you write every month. Once the money is in the "giving" account, it is untouchable for personal use. This system helps make giving a joyful experience since you won't have to fight a mental battle month after month, struggling to give out of your general account.

❑ I choose to teach this   Date Completed   _____

_____

_____

Accumulation or Utilization

Once there were two neighbors with identical cars. One of the men was extremely concerned about how much gas was in his car's tank. He would often top off the tank and was concerned about how much gas evaporated since he couldn't seem to control that factor. He never drove very far, instead he spent a lot of time at home or work thinking of ways to get more gas into the tank.

His neighbor was very different. He drove on vacation; drove to worship with people of like faith, drove on dates with his wife and drove to the donut shop with his kids.

The point of this simple story is that the first man was preoccupied with accumulating gas (money) and always making sure he had enough. The second man realized that gas (money) is not really valuable in itself. It is only valuable when it is <u>utilized</u> to accomplish things that have <u>real</u> value – things that really matter in the big picture of life. Does a larger house have real value in the bright light of a lifetime or of eternity? Probably not. Does a boat? Maybe, if it is used as the <u>means</u> to spending quantity and quality time and building your children into spiritually rich and emotionally strong adults.

In Spiritual Principles, (page 29) I say that it is worth investing some of your tank's gasoline to motivate and accomplish lasting Scripture memory. This is only one example of <u>utilizing</u> money to accomplish things that are truly valuable. (The family reading program – page 62 – will also cost something.)

Does this run counter to insurance payments, 401–Ks, college funds and mortgage payments as accumulation? No. Within a balanced perspective, these are important strategies towards utilizing the funds in the future and protecting both the "car" and the "gas tank" now.

We say hindsight is 20-20. On Monday morning it is always easy to see how you could have won the game. It is a sad sight to see a father in his 60's or 70's who wishes he would have utilized his money when he had the chance to accomplish eternal and worthwhile results. For him, the tank is now full, but the car is old and the best he can do is give his money to his kids or someone else in the hope that they will <u>use</u> it to accomplish worthwhile things.

What is your legacy? Are you utilizing what money you have to accomplish things that will last or are you hoarding the gas in your tank and fretting over the rate of evaporation?

Talk with your sons and daughters about this, maybe after they've left home, but be sure you have examples from your family history that demonstrate where you <u>utilized</u> money to achieve things that have <u>real</u> value.

❏ I choose to teach this   Date Completed   _____

_____

_____

With Few Exceptions, Take on Debt for Appreciating Assets, Save Until you can Pay Cash for Everything Else

As a borrower, I'm going to pay the full price plus interest anyway, so it is illogical to say I can't afford to pay cash. The real issue is the desire to have it now rather than later. If life simply can't go forward without this purchase, then make an exception and accept the increased cost of as small a loan as possible.

Work through this example together so they can appreciate the real increased cost.

The purchase of a car:

A Save ahead, pay cash	B Borrow now, make payments
Save $300 per month x 48 months **$ 14,400 total of your own money + 6%** average interest earned while saving	$ 16,128 borrowed now for 48 months x 10% auto loan for 48 months **$ 22,579 total of your own money**
$ 16,128 total available	

Based on this example, in Plan A you would buy the car and be half way towards paying for the next one by the time Plan B pays for the first car. Can your kids really afford to go the Plan B route?

❏ I choose to teach this   Date Completed   _____

                                                    _____

                                                    _____

Never Chase a Deal

Have you ever bought a car? A house? Have you ever sold shares of stock or shopped for a mortgage? Whether we gave it a specific name or not, most of us have at one time or another chased a deal. It goes like this: We went to the car dealer determined and able to spend no more than $10,000, but the list price was $12,900. They came down some but after 2 hours in the showroom, they threw in the extended warranty and we signed a loan for $11,900.

It works in reverse too. The house was a fair price, and mortgage rates were at about 8%. You had figured out your budget and it would work at that rate, but there was a possibility that rates might dip lower so you waited. Instead they went to 8 1/4%. It was probably only a short term jump though, so while waiting for rates to go back down below 8%, they went to 8 1/2%, so you locked in at 8 1/2%, frustrated and feeling foolish.

Here is the principle for all of us, whether it's a home, a car, or the sale of your old record collection. Do whatever research is justified given the size of the deal, and then fix a realistic buy/sell point that fits your budget or any other objectives that factor into the decision. Make that decision when you're not affected by emotion or the time pressures of the negotiating process. Then go into your deal with peace of mind and quiet assurance. There is always another car, another house, or another buyer for your record collection, but if you chase the deal, you're sure to pay more, or receive less for your sale than you planned.

P.S. If you are steadfast in your decision and refuse to chase the deal, you automatically trigger a separate principle of negotiations. Being truly willing to walk away from a deal with no purchase or sale gives you a powerful advantage because 99% of those you deal with are not willing, in the final analysis, to walk away. If your pre-determined position is realistic and fair, they'll likely give it to you when they realize you will truly walk away.

❑ I choose to teach this   Date Completed   _____

_____

_____

Managing a Checking Account / Credit Card

Help your teenager open a checking account with an ATM/debit card included. Seed the account at the beginning (if you choose) to supplement their starting funds. Give assistance and instruction, showing them how to balance the checkbook and make individual entries, but <u>never</u> fund the account after the initial set-up. Allow them to make deposits from their allowance or part-time job earnings.

Credit cards will probably have to wait until their 18th birthday. But on that 18th birthday, make it a special day. Go with them to your bank and help them apply for <u>their own</u> credit card. It is important that the card has a very low credit limit, but it must really be <u>their</u> card – not just a second name on your account. The whole point is to give them the responsibility without the safety net of dad when they rack up more charges than they can pay. (Again, the importance of the low credit limit). Just like the checking account, never fund the credit card or you have done much more damage than if you had never touched this subject at all. If you do, you'll only be demonstrating to your teen that their irresponsibility (present and future) will be solved by their dad's funds. Explain the importance of their credit rating, which they are in the process of creating. It will be essential when it comes time for a car purchase, an apartment rental, and certainly their first house purchase someday.

The purpose of these two efforts is obvious and the value is immense if lessons of family cash management can be learned when the stakes are low and there is not, as yet, a young family on the receiving end of a parent's indulgence and mismanagement.

The late Larry Burkett, financial planner and author said, "Teach these lessons to your daughter, and your future son-in-law will someday bow down and call you blessed." His statement, of course, applies equally to our boys, whose future wives will benefit or suffer from their training in this area.

❏ I choose to teach this   Date Completed   _____

_____

_____

Never Spend the Future – Selling Chickens Before they Hatch

We've all had it happen to us. In fact, it's probably the rule rather than the exception. An order comes into the company. Not a "maybe", but a solid job with a purchase order. But before you can ever count a profit, you have to endure specification changes, quantity changes, changes in your supplier costs and sometimes worst of all, collection. What appeared to be a $1,000 profit turns out to be $240 after a 120 day receivable.

This is one of those principles that everyone knows; yet most sons and daughters grow up and "spend the $1,000" only to be surprised when $240 finally comes in.

Let's agree to talk with our kids about this the first time they begin counting future earnings. Suggestion: Don't lay out the whole principle and expect them to set aside all their expectations the first time. Rather, talk a little about the possible uncertainties to come but get their projected number well established. Write it down. Then at the end of their summer job or whatever the projected time frame, revisit your discussion and the written projected profit number. They will learn by their own experience as well as your words.

❑ I choose to teach this   Date Completed   _____

_____

_____

Work and the Transition to Independence

In the first chapter of this book we used a cone to represent the decreasing amount of daily time we have to influence our kids as they get older. Ideally, there will be a converse, increasing level of personal responsibility and self sufficiency, so that leaving home at age 18 or 19 is a natural, prepared event that occurs only once and without any significant trauma.

One significant part of this transition actually begins years before leaving home when our kids can be held responsible to earn and pay part of their own expenses. At 16, they can hold a job complete with hours, deducted taxes and the need to be on time and dependable. A good way to create motivation and responsibility at this age is to make it a condition of driving the family car that they pay the increase in car insurance as we discussed earlier. I believe a car of their own at age 16 or 17 should be entirely their expense including the purchase, insurance and upkeep. If they are able to earn enough while still maintaining their grades and other commitments, the car will have created wonderful growth.

Not long ago, one of the men in our BAG (accountability) group shared a similar experience. John is a partner in an architectural firm. They often hire recent graduates with architectural degrees. He said that in his years in that position, he can just about tell the difference, without looking at the resume, between those graduates who have worked before and during their college years, and those who have never yet had to be responsible as an employee. He said, those who have had years of work experience before graduation are head and shoulders above their peers of the same age who are entering a real work environment for the first time.

Being pushed into the deep end all at once is an ineffective way to learn to swim. Let's give our kids the gift of learning financial responsibility from gradual, appropriate work experience.

❏ I choose to teach this   Date Completed   _____

_____

_____

Conclusion

We all love our kids. Every dad prays that his children will grow up to be successful and responsible in the many roles they will fill—husbands/wives, fathers/mothers, employees, leaders. But ask any dad whose kids have already left home and he'll tell you the years fly by quickly. Like our friend Tevye, that we met in chapter one, many of them could sing along with "Sunrise, sunset...Is this the little girl I carried....Wasn't it yesterday when they were small?"

Resolve today that you won't be surprised when the day comes for your children to leave the nest. Keep the 18-year-horizon in view. Resolve today that you'll choose to invest time, intentionally, to pass the baton of your experience and wisdom. Nothing could be more rewarding and fulfilling for you, and also for your kids, who will reap the benefits of your influence while avoiding many of the pitfalls that life is sure to present.

Coaches and youth leaders can be a valuable support, but you have the privilege and responsibility to be the only father that God has given to your kids.

Enjoy the process, and if you do, their leaving home one day will not be so much about leaving as it will be about transitioning to a life-long relationship of trust and replication. And with God's grace, you will live to see your own baton passed on again, to another generation.

Now get to it. Some wonderful experiences are waiting for you.

ISBN 142513065-8

Made in the USA
Lexington, KY
01 May 2014